A SEABORN VILLAGE

BORTH
A SEABORN VILLAGE

BY

TERRY DAVIES

ISBN: 0-86381-877-3

Published by
Gwasg Carreg Gwalch,
12 Iard yr Orsaf, Llanrwst, Conwy, Wales LL26 OEH.
(Tel: 01492 642031   Fax: 01492 641502)
Printed and published in Wales.

CONTENTS

ACKNOWLEDGEMENTS

I wish to acknowledge with gratitude the support, assistance or advice given by the following during the gestation of this project:

Simon Raw-Rees and Mick Kelly of Lazertran.

Myrddin ap Dafydd of Gwasg Carreg Gwalch.

Michael Freeman at the Ceredigion Museum Aberystwyth.

William Troughton, Rhydian Davies, Sarah Humphries at the National Library of Wales.

Edgar Williams and Daniel Lloyd-Williams at the Ceredigion County Library.

Helen Palmer, Glenys McBurnie and Gwyneth Roberts at the Ceredigion Archives.

Merfyn Tomos, Janet Simcox and Gwen Hough at the Merionethshire Archives, Dolgellau.

The Masons of Ffos Y Gravel Farm, the Williams and Rowlands families of Brynllys Farm, the Griffiths family of Gwastad and the Davies family of Dolclettwr Hall Farm.

Gerald Morgan, Alun and Carol Evans, Peter Glover, Paul Richards, Arthur and Elizabeth Rance-O'Dell, Hugh and Verona Hughes, Gwynfor Hughes (Castell Coch), Noreen Sharpe, Sid Clare, Stan Evans, Nick and Mary Brown, Derek and Gwen Lloyd, Mrs. Betty Doyle, Alexander "Sandy" Jones, R.A. Yates, John and Jill Matthews, Dilwyn Owen, Aran Morris, John Hughes, Anne Budge, Ronnie and Brenda Davies and Edward "Teddy" Davies.

Photographers Keith Morris, David Williams and Dr Rex Harries.

Anwen Jones for providing material on Captain David Davies.

Maisie and Jane Richards for photographic material on Captain William Richards.

Dr Reg Davies for material on the "Holt Hill".

Dr Hywel Perkins owner of the painting Holt Hill.

Finally my grateful thanks to my partner Amanda Shaw who made it all possible by being a patient typist and research assistant.

DEDICATION

This work is dedicated to the beloved memory of my grandmother Mary Davies, and Edward 'Ted' and Pamela Richards, who made it all possible.

Also to the people of Borth and its environs in Wales, who gave support, succour and love in the days of my youth. To the wonderful characters now gone, save in my dreams, who were, and are, part of the rich fabric of my experiences.

Sadly during the course of this project, two sources of Borth folklore, my uncle, David Arnold 'Defi' Davies and long time friend, John Thomas 'Jac' Richards died.

'Jac' Richards, mentioned frequently in the text, provided over the years an invaluable body of oral history and folklore. The recording of toponyms is dedicated to him. He was a folklorist, raconteur and ardent Welshman.

Er cof am hen bobl y Borth gynt.
Halen daear Cymru.

PREFACE

This work is a thumbnail sketch of Borth's historic and folkloric connection with the sea, focusing on its fisherfolk and mariners. It is also, in part, a reclamation of Borth seafarers from their hitherto subsumed role in the annals of Aberdyfi and Aberystwyth. Therefore it attempts to establish Borth's contribution to the maritime history of Wales in its own right. This account of local shipping covers the period up to the beginning of the 20th century, concentrating on the days of sail; whilst that of local fishing practices is up to the present day.

Borth's founding and its very sustenance until recently depended on the sea's piscatorial bounty. Its inhabitants became skilled in sailing Cardigan Bay waters and scouring its shores to this end. Despite being on an open storm beach with no commercial shipping facilities it still developed and sustained a strong seafaring tradition. With an average population of six hundred throughout the 19th century, the number of Borth mariners was considerable.

For years, some sixty or so old Borth skippers have been gazing out of photographs as if they too sensed that their history could be easily forgotten. These photographs are intriguing as there are no records of where the photographs have been taken, or who organised bringing the subjects together. Although there are a few Aberdyfi based captains present, I believe that the photographs were taken at Borth, as some sitters are elderly and infirm which precluded travel. Probably those from Aberystwyth or Aberdyfi came together to their native village especially for the occasion. I am sure that one photograph features John Jones (Black Jack) of the *Mervinia* and his brother David of the *Catherine Morgan*, who although Aberdyfi based were of Borth descent. Upon seeing these photographs, a few locals such as Edward "Teddy" Davies and John Hughes, confirmed my opinion that the location of three of them is outside Boston House. This ties in with the possibility that they were taken by the then chemist and amatuer photographer Mr. Williams, whose business premises were nearby.

The first author to make a meaningful mention of Borth's involvement in maritime affairs was D. W. Morgan, in his 1948 publication *'Brief Glory'*, which in essence was a history of Aberdyfi, Merionethshire. All subsequent seafaring histories of Aberdyfi are indebted to this seminal work. The next acknowledgement of Borth mariners was, again in an Aberdyfi context, in Lewis Lloyd's 1996 two-volume history of the shipping in and around the Dyfi estuary, entitled, *Aberdyfi; A Real Little Seaport*. Lloyd noted that *"Borth deserves a full length study of its own as a maritime community... comparable to that of Nefyn in Caernarvonshire"* (Lloyd, L. 1996, Vol. 1, p. 266).

It is interesting to note that in Lewis Lloyd's history of Aberdyfi there is a foreword by Professor K. O. Morgan, Queen's College, Oxford, in which he states:

> the fact that my father came from Borth, just across the Dyfi, actually strengthened the seafaring mystique since so many of Aberdyfi's mariners originated from that little sea-girt village far away in distant Cardiganshire and accessible, it seemed, only via Mr. Ellis Williams' efficient ferrying service (Lloyd, L. 1996, Vol. 1, p.5).

Here again there is mention made of Borth seafarers' important role in the Aberdyfi story. The latter part of this foreword also contains one of the reasons for Borth's neglect in terms of its maritime achievements. Borth and Aberdyfi are divided by a wide estuary, with no direct form of transport even to this day. This inconvenient separation and the expanding shipping commerce there, and at Aberystwyth were reasons enough for some Borth seafarers and their families to move to these ports. Therefore, over time, these mariners became part of the histories of Borth's two illustrious neighbours. To date the records show that of the two locations Aberdyfi was the most favoured.

It may be conjectured that around 1840 some of the village's fishermen affected by the closure of the Leri's sea mouth decided that Aberystwyth harbour was a more convenient location to operate from. This coincided with the unique Borth fishing boat design having been taken to Aberystwyth around that time. Later on, allowing for the vagaries of maritime employment there was a discernable movement of mariners from Borth to Aberdyfi in the 1860's in response to that port's slate export boom. As a result of the maritime expansion in the 19th century there was a marked increase in the numbers of master mariners from Borth. The village womenfolk were also to play an important role in shipping affairs.

By 1900, with Aberdyfi's decline as a port, some Borth men moved permanently to places such as Liverpool or Middlesborough. Others relocated to Barry or Manchester, lured by job prospects there because Borth's Richard Davies was dock master at Barry and another villager, Richard Williams of Britannia House had taken charge of the Manchester Ship Canal. However the prodigious numbers of mariners emanating from the village meant that the majority of seafarers still used Borth as a home base well into the middle of the 20th century.

Prior to the beginning of this project I went on a sail training course on the barquentine *One and All,* whose home port, and my current place of residence, is Adelaide in South Australia. A week's voyaging in the Southern Ocean gave one an idea of conditions experienced by Borth mariners in the 19th century. Australia has six sailing ships based in various ports that offer such experiences. It is my fervent wish that Wales should have a sail training ship, possibly a topsail schooner that would visit every Welsh port for a term of residence.

This historical sketch is not in any way intended to be a full scale study of the village, but hopefully will contribute in part to a more complete history of Borth.

TERRY DAVIES,
BRYNOWEN COTTAGE, BORTH.
APRIL 2003

HISTORY

Borth is the northernmost coastal village in Ceredigion, formerly Cardiganshire, and lies in the parish of Llanfihangel Genau'r Glyn. It encompasses two townships, Cyfoeth y Brenin and Henllys. These confusingly termed townships were simply divisions within parishes and have nothing to do with towns as we know them. The village includes the hamlets of Glanwern, Penbont, Dolybont and Ynyslas as well as the farms contained in Cyfoeth y Brenin and Henllys. Borth straddles a shingle bank formed between the sea and a large fenland, which is called Cors Fochno, traditionally thought to mean the Fenland of Pigs. According to folklore:

A prince who lived well to the south of the Borth area decided to take stock of his realm. The prince's entourage travelled with their own food supplies, amongst which were pigs. A large tract of marshland marked the northern boundary of his domain and, according to the story, when he arrived the locals there had never seen pigs before, so to commemorate this wonder they named the fen Cors Fochno to mark the event.

Perhaps what can be read from this is that these were the first domesticated pigs the locals had seen, as opposed to the abundant wild boar that roamed ancient Wales. This prince may have been Gwaethfoed who gave his name to a rocky outcrop in the fenland near Borth called Ynys Gwaethfoed (Gwaethfoed's Island). His descendants supposedly began the Pryse dynasty of Gogerddan estate. He lived in the Vale of Aeron and claimed descent from Gwyddno Garanhir (Gwyddno Longshanks). The latter's name resonates through the early history of the north Ceredigion coast.

Exactly how and when Borth came into being is lost in the mists of the distant past well before written history. Its first inhabitants may have settled in the area farming the high ground and fishing the sea, especially for herring which must have been abundant well before Borth's establishment. It has been conjectured that a sea port called Hafan Gwyddno or Porth Gwyddno mentioned in ancient texts is Borth and that the submerged lands of Cardigan Bay near the village were referred to as Maes Gwyddno (Gwyddno's Meadow), (North, 1957, p175). By the Middle Ages there were a few permanent dwellings tucked on the sea edge on the southern high ground and possibly others on the shingle bank that ran northwards.There may have also been dwellings around the old Leri river mouth as both Borth and Aberleri are named in the late 14th century.

Large groups of seasonal herring fishermen had been drawn to north Ceredigion waters for centuries. This is in accordance with later descriptions of the area in Elizabethan times, when Borth and the Dyfi were mentioned as gathering places for such fishing fleets. Boats could shelter on the beach from the easterlies that blow in the autumn, especially inside Trwyn Cyntaf (First Point), a much more convenient arrangement than negotiating the Dyfi bar. This long established practice may have given this area with its little gathering of dwellings the name Borth which is from 'porth'... harbour; in the context of it meaning shelter. It has only been spelt Porth on rare occasions as in the maps of Thomas Kitchen 1765 and J. Roper 1805.

Borth and Aberleri are named for the first time in a church terrier dated 1373. Also mentioned in the same document are the turbaries, peat digging rights, on Cors Fochno which the church kept for centuries until their sale in the 1960s. All this was written in Latin, and is contained in the Llanfihangel Castell Gwallter parochial records, which stated:

Decimae Halecis Pertinentis Ad Borth Et Aberlery (Bygones, 1876, p. 28)

The Castell Gwallter in the church name comes from a nearby castle site near Blaenwaun Farm. At the very edge of a massive drop into the Llandre valley are the remains of a moat and bailey earthwork castle called Castell Gwallter, which means Walter's Castle. It was built by Walter De Bec during the Norman ascendancy in Ceredigion, between 1110 - 1135. Often attacked by the Welsh, it was razed to the ground in 1136 by Owain and Cadwaladr, princes of North Wales. After rebuilding, the princes of South Wales, Cadell, Maredudd and Rhys, attacked it persistently and finally, in 1153, Rhys and Maredudd completely destroyed the structure to prevent re-garrisoning by the Normans. The nearby spring that was its water supply on the high escarpment still exists to this day. Llanfihangel Castell Gwallter is the old name for the church, but since Tudor times it has been known as Llanfihangel Genau'r Glyn (St Michaels at the Mouth of the Glen).

In the past, Borth was in the township of Cyfoeth y Brenin, and the northern part, built on the shingle bank, was known as Morfa Borth (Borth Seamarsh) in the township of Henllys. Nowadays, Borth has become Upper Borth, and Morfa Borth is now Borth. In the 1880s when there were 20 boats fishing from the village, many were kept on the shingle bank between today's Evelwen and Beach Cottage. In the Llanfihangel church records and the account books of a local Friendly Society called the Castell Gwallter Ivorites, there is a further division of the village, namely Gwastad Borth. This was the meadow land that included the then Pengoitan Farm and today's Gwastad, Brynrodyn and Pengraig Farms.

Many villages on the Ceredigion seaboard developed around religious sites such as Llanon, Llangrannog and Llanrhystyd; or castle sites such as those of Cardigan and Aberystwyth. Borth did not, and so it is not surprising that there has always been a folkloric supposition that the village's founding was by outcasts from the social constraints prevalent in ancient times. It is a settlement largely independant of church, castle or manor house and its small fishing community was founded, so folklore tells us, by Teulu Sion Dafydd... John Davies' family. The author D. W. Morgan, whose parents were of Borth stock, says he was descended from a branch of this Borth family, namely that of Will Sion Dafydd, on his mother's side, and he says:

If all were known these successive Sion Dafydds would extend back hundreds of years, maybe casting nets off Borth shore, and killing mawn on Cors Fochno before history was (Morgan, D. W., 1948, P. 261).

In this quotation, "killing mawn" is confusing. Digging peat, in Welsh is lladd mawn, which literally translates into killing peat. Therefore, Morgan has resorted to using English and Welsh in the same phrase. The notion of the predominence of a Davies clan in Borth may have occurred more recently, around the end of the 18th century, as the names of villagers recorded in documents dated 1565, 1678 and 1745 do not support this supposition. The Rees, Williams, Daniel, Jones, Hughes, James, Lewis, Lloyd and Richards families were also prominent in Borth's shipping affairs

The uncertainties concerning Borth's origin fuel speculation and beg many questions. When did settlement occur and where did the first inhabitants come from? Were they a mix of the old inhabitants and the Celts prior to the arrival of the

Romans? Could they be the remnants of Cunedda's army who had come to Wales from South Scotland to rid the coastal plains of the Goedelic presence in the 6th century? Did people settle the area during the time of Cunedda's son Ceredig, who gave his name to the county? Or was it later that a beachside settlement began at Borth in 1206 confident of survival because fish, presumably herrings, were plentiful at this time in the Aberystwyth area? It was recorded in *The Chronicle of the Princes* in that year that *"God gave an abundance of fish in the estuary of the Ystwyth"* (Smylie M. 1998, p.52). Many places must have been established prior to being recorded by name or marked on a map. Estuaries and river mouths were settled by the earliest humans in Wales as they provided an abundant source of food that was reasonably accessible. Even in ancient times the kings of Ceredigion were seafarers. Gwgawn ap Meurig, better known as Gwgawn 'Cleddfrudd' (bloodsword) is believed to have drowned in 872 on a sea voyage (Kirby, 1970, p.268).

Ancient historical events are associated with the Borth area, such as the Battle of Cors Fochno which took place sometime before the Norman invasion of 1066. There are different versions, but the most likely is a Welsh power struggle where Caradoc ap Rhydderch ap Iestin sought the help of the Saxon King Harold Godwinson, and his brother Tostig to defeat King Griffith ap Llewelyn ap Seisyllt of North Wales. The armies met at the coastal junction between north and south Wales, obviously the Dyfi estuary, where Tostig's troops were joined by a sea force commanded by Harold. The battle's location points to the southern shore in the vicinity of Cors Fochno (Arch. Camb. 1851, pp 210-215). They could hardly fight on the marshland itself, so the foreshore and the beaches at Borth and Ynyslas are likely locations.

Much of Wales' early history is contained in its poetry. In the Borth context a poem attributed to Bleddyn Ddu written around 1090 mentions the battle of Cors Fochno which had occurred 30 years previously. In a treatise written in 1851 by T. Stephens, it states in the author's footnotes that he does not know where the places 'Eleri' or 'Chwilfynydd' mentioned in the poem are situated (Arch Camb. 1851, pp. 204-219). Eleri is surely the Leri river which flowed through Cors Fochno in ancient times to enter the sea on a wide stretch of beach that would have been ideal as a landing place for a sea force. 'Chwilfynydd' may have been the original name, or a poetically convenient form for Yr Wylfa. Later in another instance the poet Ffylip Brydydd was describing the scene to the south of Aberdyfi at Borth in lines fifteen and sixteen of his praise poem to prince Rhys Gryg, sixth son of the Lord Rhys? The poem mentions waves breaking on the shingle bank at Porth Gwyddno which is a reference to Rhys Gryg having been at Aberdyfi in the winter of 1216 when the lands of Deheubarth were settled amongst the princes of south Wales. (Costigan, et al., 1995, p.174-8). This prince died fighting the English in 1233.

In *Brut y Tywysogion* (*Chronicle of the Princes*) 1109, it was recorded that Cadwgan ap Bleddyn and his son Owain, after an escapade by the latter at Cenarth Bychan near Cardigan, journeyed to the Dyfi upon hearing that an Irish trading ship was anchored there, so that they could board her to seek refuge in Ireland. This episode came about because Owain had been smitten by the beauty of his cousin Nest, who unfortunately for him, was married to Gerald de Windsor, a Norman and friend of King Henry I (1100-35). Owain with his cohorts set about abducting her, and would probably have killed her husband to boot, if Nest had not guided him to safety. The outcome of this reckless shortlived abduction was that Owain, his father and their companions had to escape swiftly northwards. The chronicler does not mention Borth, but they probably boarded their escape ship from the southern side as it was possibly anchored on the Borth side of the estuary within hailing distance in the deeper water. They would surely have headed for the river mouth along the shingle strand and dunes in case they missed the vessel. D.W. Morgan speculated that this ship had been far up river, probably to Llyn Bwtri, an anchorage near where a medieval manor house stood (Morgan, D. W. 1948. p 5).

Gerald de Windsor and Nest, were the grandparents of Giraldus Cambrensis, Gerallt Gymro, Gerald the Welshman 1146-1223 who left a dynamic and invaluable record of 12th century Wales. This loquacious churchman left an account of a mission he undertook with Archbishop Baldwin in 1188 to raise men for the crusades; The Journey Through Wales. In his journal he mentions the crossing of the Dyfi with this minuscule description of the event:

... we crossed the River Dovey and so came to the territory of the sons of Cynan. (Thorpe, 1998, p. 181).

This is one of the rare instances when, unfortunately for posterity, he forsook his garrulousness. Another of his works, *The Description of Wales*, gives details of the appearance of ordinary Welsh people and a day to day account of their lives, as well as the flora and fauna of Wales, including a mention of beavers on the river Teifi.

At that time Aberdyfi meant simply the mouth of the Dyfi, as there was as yet no such settlement as Aberdyfi. In all probability only a ferryman's abode and an inn existed at the site until the 1700s. Borth was seldom mentioned in connection with the ferry crossing as somewhere along Traeth Maelgwyn lay the southern ferry landing place. From there a track led past Moelynys and on to Borth, a mile south along the shingle bank. In the 18th century the Dyfi estuary with its developing small anchorages such as Carreg that facilitated the export produce of local mines often warranted more cartographic attention than the small farms and fishermen's cottages, a few miles away, that constituted Borth.

There is a presumption that the only Dyfi crossing point was at the end of the track along the shingle bank where Borth stood, or where it would stand, and from this travellers such as the Lord Rhys in 1156 and Giraldus Cambrensis in 1188 would therefore have travelled through the village. This is problematic as the Dyfi estuary is vast and could have had other crossing places elsewhere up the estuary for larger bands of travellers. It is more than likely that both the Lord Rhys and Geraldus Cambrensis with their respective entourages crossed the Dyfi by fording it well up the estuary near Machynlleth. It would be a few more centuries before there was a sizeable ferry at the rivermouth for carrying horses and farm livestock

However small groups or lone travellers journeying north used the track down from Rhydypennau or the coastal road from Clarach over Rhiw Fawr. Another way was to follow the route from Llandre church over the top via Cilolwg and Rhiwlas farms, down Lon Goed to Borth and along the strand to the Dyfi. Of all the possible access points on the southern side of the estuary, the shortest ferry boat crossing was at the end of the Borth/Ynyslas route, especially for the mariners of Borth who had to access the port facilities of Aberdyfi from the 18th century onwards. T. Wynne Thomas's history of the ferry maintains that this route had existed and been controlled since ancient times by either the ruling princes of Wales, the crown, church or the gentry. In the 15th century the lessee, under the Crown was Jenkin ap Iorwerth of Ynys y Maengwyn. The ferry boat crossing was between today's Aberdyfi and the pebbly beach site opposite, called Cerrig y Penrhyn.

In the 14th century, whilst waiting to be ferried southwards from Merionethshire to join his beloved, poet Dafydd ap Gwilym became a little exasperated with the vagaries of the weather affecting the ferry service across the hazardous Dyfi when he chides the

Curly-topped, loud-crying wave,
Bar not, fair hopes my passage
To that shore, where waits my reward,
Make no delay, no hindrance.
                    ("The Wave on the River Dyfi"
                        by Dafydd ap Gwilym)

This poem's reference to rough seas affecting the ferry service confirms that the location of the crossing was at the river mouth.

Even though for centuries royalty or religious orders had fishing rights over rivers, estuaries and beaches, there were still some stretches of the coastline not under their governance. Subsistence sea fishing was probably undertaken free of any impost in medieval Wales, other than in major centres like Aberystwyth, where it was a well organised industry. In outlying areas it was left to the parish churches' discretion to collect nominal tithes as indicated by the Llanfihangel church terrier of 1373. The surrounding countryside was controlled, and therefore, idyllic in the eyes of landowners and the clergy. The beach area was another matter; it was covered in water twice a day and those that chose to live with this instability were possibly viewed as also being unstable in the scheme of things. Until recently the beach has often been demonised as the place of invasion and, in peace time, of idlers and social outcasts. There was outrage seven centuries ago when fisherman in Wales traded on the beach in an attempt to avoid paying their dues. There, the fishermen presumed they were beyond the periphery of any financial impositions as: *"In 1302, fishermen were being fined for selling herring below the high water mark to escape paying market tolls"* (Smylie, M. 1998, p.52).

Prior to Elizabethan times, the western coastal areas of Britain, including Wales, had been neglected as far as any regulatory authority was concerned. Not only was there a need to tighten up this loose end of the realm in terms of the rampant piracy occuring there, but a survey was essential to assess its shipping; especially its naval and military potential for defence purposes. Slave trading was probably another concern of the authorities, although it is doubtful that the slavers reached as far as Ceredigion. The Romans, known to have taken slaves from all parts of Britain, were not the only people to ply this trade. Up to Elizabethan times and into the early Stuart period, Moroccan pirates raided south and west Britain and Southern Ireland for slaves; especially fair-haired and light skinned women and children (Gater. D. 1992, p 15). In the mid 16th century for the first time, there was to be a county by county survey of the Welsh coastline instigated by Elizabeth I, whereby her Privy Council appointed permanent Commissions for each maritime county. These surveys were conducted in 1555-6 and 1557-8 and were presented to the Piracy Commission. This resulted in the English customs system arriving in Wales, and from this came the Welsh Port Books, which are a reference source for the maritime history of the principality from the 16th century onwards. From these Elizabethan surveys comes another mention of Borth, in a quote from the report on Havens and Creeks of the County of Cardigan, (1565):

Item theris also too smale landinge places Borthe and Divi, beinge in the maner of Generglin, John Ougan esquier under the quenes maiesties lord and owener therof (Lewis, 1927,p.31).

This John Ougan also deputed Thomas Jenkin and John Vaughan ap Redderch to keep an eye on *"the haven of Divi and Borth"*. Who was this John Ougan? It has been suggested that he may have been John Wogan of Wiston Pembrokeshire, who owned land in north Ceredigion. He was the grandson of Maud Clement, descended from Geoffrey Clement, who received extensive lands between the Dyfi and Rhydypennau. John Wogan sold them to John Pryse of Gogerddan in 1568 (G. Morgan, pers. comm, 2003).

In Tudor times the majority of local vessels plying the Ceredigion coast did not exceed 5 tons and were engaged in coastal trading and herring fishing. This had grave implications for the defence of the realm as witnessed by the formulation of the Piracy Commissions mentioned previously. Such concerns were no doubt fuelled by the type of incident that occurred near Borth in 1597. For many years after the defeat of the Spanish Armada there were recurring incidents of Spanish raiders making the odd punitive attack that saw places such as Penzance and Plymouth torched. One such raider hove to in the Dyfi for 10 days. The militia of both counties, Ceredigion and Merionethshire, failed to capture or destroy her as there was a shortage of manpower in the Dyfi estuary region at this time. The site of the future port of Aberdyfi only had a few houses which served the ferry route and there were certainly no naval warships to challenge the intruder. A single small cannon fired from the land would have sunk her, or at least disabled her, but she made good her escape. This ship was called the Bear of Amsterdam, and later surrendered off Dartmouth, devoid of ammunition and short on food. To restock provisions and avoid conflict was probably the reason for the Dyfi stopover (Morgan, D. W., 1948, pp 11-15).

The first substantial mention of Borth's inhabitants and their occupation is in a document dated 1678 titled *A list of seafaring men, boatmen and bargemen from the county of Cardigan taken the 18th day of May 1678*. Both townships, or in this list parishes, that comprise Borth, Cyfoeth y Brenin and Henllys, are mentioned. The names, ages and marital status of the men are provided. They are all noted as being at home so we may presume that some others were away at sea. In Henllys there were Hugh Richards 60 years of age, John Roignald 43, William Morgan 50, Hugh Owen 30, Richard Morris 24 and Morris Evan 40. In Cyfoeth y Brenin there was a Hugh David Lloyd 63, William Thomas 58, Hugh ap Evan 40, Morgan Richards 38, Richard Davies 56, Morris David Lloyd 40, Morgan Thomas 31 and Lewis Humphrey 49. In total the Borth area had 14 fishermen at this time, whilst Aberystwyth, a much larger place, had 19, and Cardigan had only 4, the same number as tiny Clarach. The ages of the fishermen indicate that the majority were middle-aged and older. (N.L.W. Mss. 3277). This confirms that fishing was an activity taken up primarily by retired seafarers. However, so important to the wellbeing of the village was the herring that even into the 20th century, many mariners in the ocean-going and coastal trade arranged to be home in the autumn for the piscatorial harvest. The discrepancy between the number of fishermen in Cardigan and Aberystwyth in this survey may be because those at Cardigan were involved in netting salmon and sewin along the river Teifi, whereas more men and seagoing boats were needed to chase the vast shoals of herring in the Aberystwyth area.

On the 22nd of November 1746 an unexpected cargo came to the village when a Portuguese ship ran aground at Trwyn Pellaf (Far Point), the tidal rockshelf at the southern end of Borth. Depositions were made to the Gogerddan Estate by local witnesses and salvagers which recorded that:

David James, David Lewis and Edward Williams, all of Borth did help to secure severall Puncheon of oyle Lemons orange Chest Pomgranets Ropes Corkwood and one sayle… stranded on ye shore within ye Lordships of John Pugh Pryce (Jenkins, 1950-51, p.198)

This story may have boosted tales in the area which claim that many of the swarthier coastal dwellers were the descendants of crew members from wrecked European ships. Another more grisly tale possibly linked to the 1746 Portuguese wreck has come to light in a letter from A. C. Vaughan to J. Glyn Davies, dated 19th September, 1913 (N.L.W. Mss. 644). In this correspondence Vaughan was relating a story of how, when approaching Aberystwyth harbour by sea, he witnessed a screaming match between the masters of an outward bound Borth vessel and an inbound Aberystwyth craft after a near miss at the harbour entrance. The witness heard the word Portuguese, which sent the Borth man into a frenzy. Vaughan, upon landing, sought out the Aberystwyth skipper and enquired as to the cause of the commotion, especially the Borth man's reaction to the word Portuguese. He was told that Borth men were cursed until the ninth generation by a dying Portuguese sailor who had been washed ashore half drowned. This foreigner had been set upon by Borth folk for his boots. Because the boots were waterlogged and tight, the locals cut off his legs to get them and left him on the beach. Because the Portuguese was dying, he cursed the perpetrators for nine generations (Vaughan, 1913, Corr. 644, N.L.W.). Was this particular sailor from the 1746 wreck and did such skulduggery go on that was not reported to the local squire at Gogerddan?

A variation of this tale maintains that the Portuguese sailor was chased northwards by the villagers until he was eventually caught and murdered near today's Ynyslas road bridge. Apparently for a time after this event any stranger was called a Portuguese (S.Evans and S.Clare, pers comm, 2003). There are reverberations of this event mentioned in an 1875 edition of Bygones. The article's author had met with an Aberdyfi man who had been badly frightened one night by seeing lights on the other side of the estuary moving from Borth northwards toward the sandhills opposite. It was reported that:

> He evidently considered them of supernatural origin as he told me an incoherent story of a boat's crew of shipwrecked foreigners having been murdered when they came ashore there many years ago. (Upon further enquiry, I find there was some tradition of the sort) (Holland. 1992, p. 109)

In Ceredigion up until the 17th century there were few substantial centres of population. Apart from Aberystwyth and Cardigan, it was mainly a scattering of small hamlets and villages. Huge areas of the county had no hedges or fences up until 1800, from which time the best of this open land was rapidly enclosed. Land such as the narrow Morfa Borth shingle strip was not highly prized as it had scant pasture and was prone to sea encroachment and marshland flooding in winter. It also had a centuries' old track through it to the ferry point at Ynyslas, so settlement on the Morfa would have been of no great concern. It is more than likely that some of the first fisherfolks' dwellings at this site were seasonal shelters that later became permanent.

Folklore maintains that some were built utilising the *ty unnos* (one-night house) system. This tradition, dating from the Middle ages, meant a person could construct a dwelling on common land overnight. There would be little objection from surrounding landowners as the 'land' in this case, a stone strand, was a useless possession as far as food production was concerned. The ty unnos structure had to have its own roof in place and smoke coming out of a hole in it by dawn of the next day. Apparently at Borth temporary walls were built of peat blocks, as there was an inexhaustible supply at adjacent Cors Fochno. The occupant would mark the boundary of his new acquisition by throwing an axe and where it landed delineated the margins of the new property. Whether this demarcation tradition was used in Borth is as speculative as whether any one night houses were actually erected. Once the process of entitlement was established by living a year and a day in the dwelling, the owner could then rebuild the walls from packed earth or the more substantial beach stones. Early dwellings were turf roofed or thatched with bullrushes from the adjacent marshland, and were internally partitioned with wattle and daub. The widespread use of slate during the industrial revolution eventually heralded the demise of the age-old turf or thatched roofing of dwellings in west Wales.

By the beginning of the 19th century Borth had grown considerably, especially the northern part known then as Morfa Borth. The tithe maps of the early 19th century show a considerable number of dwellings on the seaward side of Borth's only main street, beyond the grasp of tithe gatherers, which validates the folkloric notion of a feisty independence. All twenty or so of these had no land whatsoever, giving another reason for non-inclusion in the tithes. All were owner-occupied suggesting that the one night house system may have been practiced in Borth. Fourteen were occupied by mariners' widows, indicating the perilous nature of seafaring. The number of widows appropriately dressed in mourning black gave rise to the expression Brain y Borth (Borth Crows), which was eventually extended to include any Borth person who expressed a spirited independence.

Here we may consider the remark made by the Reverend D.T. Hughes in his series of articles that appeared in the *Cambrian News* sporadically from April to December of 1947, entitled 'Looking Back'. He stated that there were no dwellings on the seaside of Borth's main road one hundred years prior to 1947, which meant 1847. The tithe map of 1841 contradicts this statement. However there may have been a time much earlier when dwellings were predominantly on the land side of the road, a safe distance from sea encroachment. This also meant that they were slightly sheltered from the prevailing southwesterlies by the high shingle bank. In some areas the rows of cottages were side on to the coastline, which meant that any heavy seas broaching the shingle bank would flow past the cottages down to the marshland causing minimal damage. Examples are at today's White Lion Place, Craigfryn and Ty Cerrig. It was the more intrepid who built on the seaward side.

Borth residents, though dependent upon the sea, knew its many moods and how treacherous it could become in the blink of an eye. This was evident in the design and construction of their cottages. Nowadays many of the houses backing onto the sea have changed in architectural character with the addition of verandas which was unheard of in the old days. From around the mid 1800s slate took over as the preferred roofing material and the cottages with their backs to the sea used it on roofs that sloped right down almost to the ground. This proved a useful defence when huge seas crashed against the back of the village. We may conjecture that against the common 'enemy' the villagers huddled together architecturally as well as socially. Despite every effort, nature proved more powerful time and time again. One of the worst storms recorded was in 1896. The gale-driven high tide on the 8th of October 1896, swamped the village destroying five dwellings at the southern end and severly damaging a dozen others (*Cambrian News*, October, 1896).

Some cottages near the southern end had compacted earth walls which are still there beneath a cement render finish, such as today's Journeys End and West Winds. Apparently there were others in a ruined state opposite Wesley Chapel on the seaside in the 1920s (A. Morris, pers. comm. 2003). Intriguingly, earth walled houses were obviously preferred by some despite being at risk from sea damage, probably because they were warmer to live in than the stone walled ones. It was a well understood building technique brought by those who had moved from the surrounding high ground onto the Morfa. Often wall construction was a combination of both materials, stone and earth. One such earth walled cottage can be seen in the background of the photograph captioned *Native Captains, Borth,* on the site of today's Glan yr Aig. It is interesting to note that D.W. Morgan refers to Borth cottages as; *"white-washed wattle tenements"* (Morgan, 1948, p.196) and another author commenting on an 1834 depiction of Aberdyfi says that the wattle walled cottages there were buttressed by having large slabs of stone laid against them (Lewis, 2001, p.2). One speculates that if wattle dwellings had to be supported in the sheltered environs of Aberdyfi, then surely wattle cottages at Borth would have been short lived considering their vulnerable position at the sea edge.

Many of Borth's cottages were rebuilt in the latter half of the 19th century, to be recreated as two or three-storied Victorian houses. An example is today's Morwylfa in the centre of the village which was once the site of an old stone cottage. This little dwelling was a hive of activity at one time as its retired sea captain owner, Thomas Davies of the sloop Venus, used to sound a bell to gather villagers together to hear important news. Captain Davies was born around 1800 and lived through the Napoleonic Wars where a cousin or uncle of his, Moses Davies of Borth had been press-ganged to fight the French. Borth residents had to visit the cottage of Ann 'Gazette' to learn how their investments or loved ones fared, since she subscribed to the Shipping News and charged others to read it. Many other cottages including those built of mud and thatch have long since vanished.

It was in such dwellings that seafaring families were raised, many of whom were matriarchal because of the frequently long absences of the men. In such circumstances women had to head the household, especially when, if widowed, they had the added responsibility of becoming part or sole owner of a vessel. Borth's maritime culture, cemented over the generations, engendered a degree of stoicism amongst the womenfolk who were often the business brain as well as the heart of the family. Even as early as the 1760s, records show that Borth woman, Jane Pugh had half ownership in a sloop. A century later in 1871 Ann Jenkins, wife of master mariner Lewis Jenkins, became the sole owner of the barque Dorothy after her husband's death. Her nephew Captain John Jones took over the running of this vessel. Although only 32 years of age he was already an experienced seaman having captained the schooner Glad Tidings in 1865 and the barque Alice in 1869. In 1881 Elizabeth Rees, widow of Captain David Rees, ran the barque Drusus with the financial help of two other local women. One senses the strength within the old Borth community where everyone worked for each other's mutual benefit, forged by the vicissitudes of seafaring. By the end of the 19th century, the wealth accumulated through shipping endeavours was reflected in better social conditions and improved housing.

The pace of village life which had remained unchanged for centuries quickened from around 1840, boosted twenty years later by the arrival of the railway. The age old pastoral time-clock of the seasons was now at an end. A day's end at Borth in the autumnal herring season prior to this change has been described thus:

Soft soft as rabbit paws, the twilight clustered around the little curve of cottages, and dim candlelight winked and twinked from the quartered windows. Slowly the day put on the sables of the night and stole away, widow quiet, in the cortege of the sun (Richards. 1948, p.1).

1. Looking north from Craigfryn, 1890

2. Looking south opposite Evelwen, 1890

3. View looking north from Fron field, circa 1890

4. Upper Borth, circa 1910

FISHTRAPS AND FOLKLORE

Tradition has it that the boulder-strewn formation exposed at low water immediately to the south of the causeway at Wallog contains an ancient gored, which is the Welsh name for a fish trap or weir. Massive boulders and pole fences were formed into walls to create triangular, circular or oval *goredi*. At Aberarth and Morfa Mawr, twenty miles to the south of Borth, there are several well preserved medieval goredi. Around that time, Aberarth was a grange and small port for the inland Cistercian Abbey of Strata Florida. Some of these weirs were still in use up until the early years of the 20th century.

The word Wallog may mean unusual, quirky or not quite right. Obviously the phenomenon of the causeway promoted otherworld possibilities. Such feelings still spring to the forefront of the mind as at low water the bouldered causeway seems to beckon one to walk on its dreamlike surface over the sea and out beyond the horizon. Such notions also occur when walking amongst the remains of the sunken forest often exposed on Borth beach. Others maintain that Wallog is a man's name, Gwallawg (the hairy one) who figures in early Welsh poetry (G. Morgan, pers. comm., 2003). This is Gwallog ap Lleenog who came to Wales from the north of Britain towards the end of the 6th century and was mentioned in a poetic dialogue between Gwyddno Garanhir and Gwyn ap Nudd (Stephens, 1853, pp.43-62). He is supposedly buried at Llanddeiniol.

The gored at Wallog is far older than any of those at Morfa Mawr and has traditionally been attributed to Gwyddno Garanhir. If this is so, then it is the one mentioned in *The Book of Taliesin* that was entwined with the *Mabinogion* stories. *Mabinogion* is a pluralised version of the original term mabinogi, which means boyhood, thus Tales of Boyhood. It may also mean the tales that an apprentice poet or story teller had to know. The *Mabinogion* and associated stories are a collection of tales originating from the 11th and 12th centuries; concentrating on the coastal regions of Wales. They were the accumulation of much older stories from the dawn of Celtic civilisation, brilliantly elaborated and embellished by the Welsh. Compiled by Lady Charlotte Guest, from ancient texts, these tales eventually appeared in print in the 19th century. Due to the great age of their settings, geophysical differences are detectable, especially pertaining to sea level changes.

Evidence of sea level changes conjure up mythologies concerning ships plying the old Celtic sea routes. There are references to a kind of floating world, where there were hallucinatory sightings of strange ships and improbable crews plying the shallow seas between Wales and Ireland. There had been a centuries old connection between the Welsh and the Irish across the short stretch of sea that divides their respective lands. During the Norman conquest many Welsh princes took refuge in Ireland. From the 17th century onwards Irish imports such as nets and salt were important for the development of Ceredigion's herring industry. Another outcome of this Celtic trading alliance cemented down the centuries are references to the high regard that Welsh mariners had for their Irish counterparts. The fact that Welsh sailors chose, of all the world's nationalities, to have an Irishman with them on the yardarm in perilous conditions encountered on sailing ships is proof of this. This is referred to not only in local Borth stories, but can be found in D.W. Morgan's Brief Glory and also in a letter that appeared in *Maritime Wales* (no.4, p.128).

In ancient and medieval Wales, coastal fishtraps were quite common. Some of these have been fished successfully up until the 1900s. At the Rhos Fynach (Monks Meadow) gored, built around 1200, near the Little Orme, north Wales, they caught 35,000 herring on a single tide in 1850, and ten tons of mackerel were caught overnight in 1907. When these structures were located far from an abbey site, weir wardens were appointed to look after them. The gored of Gwyddno Garanhir is reputed to have produced a valuable catch on every May Eve. The *Book of Taliesin* refers to its location as being on a strand between the Dyfi and Aberystwyth (Guest, 1997, p.190). In his essay *Taliesin and the Borth Weir* D.W. Morgan favours a Borth location, but as the shoreline has changed he conjectures that it is now beneath the sea. However for centuries the Wallog location features in local tradition. It is between the Dyfi and Aberystwyth, with a strand in the form of the causeway Sarn Cynfelin, and has obviously older weir remains than the Cistercian ones at Aberarth. Sarn Cynfelin means Cynfelin's causeway; he was a Welsh born saint descended from Cunedda. He also gave his name to the ancient church two miles inland from Ynyslas called Llangynfelin, as well as the now vanished coastal chapel between Wallog and Clarach, called Capel Cynfelin. There are areas in the Clarach Valley that also bear his name.

If Gwyddno's gored is the one at Wallog, then he may have had his fort or manor house on the high hill of Moelcerni, or somewhere between Wallog and Clarach. Another contender is today's nearby underwater mound of stones just offshore, called Tol Faer (Fort Mound). This may have been a substantial mound at the end of a small causeway extending from the bouldery ground under the adjacent cliffs 16 centuries ago. Owing to erosion it appears only as a stony protrusion above sea level on an 1841 map and thereafter to disappear . These conjectured locations are within a mile of the weir, which would always have been in view. There are tantalising poetic references to places associated with the name Cynfelin. Little Gwion, who transmogrified into Taliesin, was questioned by King Maelgwyn as to his identity. The poetic child prodigy answered in the form of a riddle poem, where one line stated, *"I have been on the White Hill, in the court of Cynvelyn"* (Graves, 1971, p.81). Centuries later, a place called Capel Cilvellen, Cynfelin? sometimes spelt with a 'k', appears on old maps marked as being on the hill between Wallog and Clarach. Perhaps its occupants built the Wallog weir, or they may have, as was common practice, rebuilt an older weir that was already in place, in that instance Gwyddno Garanhir's fishtrap.

Other than the piscatorial element of Gwyddno's gored, there is the associated legend concerning the Welsh poet Taliesin (Radiant Brow). The infant Taliesin had been cast, Moses-like, into the sea in a small coracle which drifted with the tide to eventually become trapped in Gwyddno's gored. Taliesin's story is an example of the beauty of ancient Welsh folk tales. This is the version I know:

> *Ceridwen, wife of Tegid Foel, became a witch so as to give her ugly son Morfran some compensatory gifts. A cauldron was to be kept boiling for a year and a day whilst she searched the countryside for special herbs to compound a magic potion. This potion would change Morfran into a brilliant handsome individual. Blind Morda and Gwion Bach were given the task of cauldron minding. Eventually during this task three drops of the potion flew out and one landed on Gwion's finger. To soothe the scald he instinctively put it in his mouth which meant that he now had the magic power intended for Morfran. Rightly fearing Ceridwen's wrath he took advantage of his newly acquired powers and changed into a hare, whereupon she became a greyhound. He hastily changed into a fish and took to the river; Ceridwen now chased him as an otter. Gwion, now desperate, turned into a bird; but she became a hawk. Terrified, he turned into a grain of wheat, whereupon Ceridwen changed into a black crested hen and ate him. Nine months later she gave birth, but could not find it in her heart to kill the tiny infant. Ceridwen put him in a leather bag, placed him in a coracle and cast him into the sea, where fate saw him caught in Gwyddno's gored. It was Gwyddno's son Elfin who found him. Hitherto Elfin had been a luckless lad, so much so that his father let him mind the gored on the always bountiful eve of May. Unbelievably,*

and to the weir warden's disgust, the only thing caught was a small coracle - but what a catch! It was the infant that not only changed Elfin's luck but became one of the great poets of Britain, Taliesin.

There are variations to the Taliesin story, depending on where the storyteller located the weir site. In another Borth version Elfin marries Angharad, daughter of Seithenin, who caused Cantre Gwaelod to be flooded. Elfin, now landless, ekes out a living keeping bees on Cors Fochno and trapping salmon around the Dyfi. He makes a cunning fishtrap near his home. One night, Angharad, hearing strange sounds, goes to the weir and finds the baby Taliesin there in a coracle. He is adopted and becomes Britain's greatest bard, and when he dies he is buried near Borth, above the village honouring his name, Taliesin. One can easily adapt this story to a specific location at Borth in the following speculative scenario: Elfin and Angharad's home is on Ynys Dwrgi. The surrounding fenland of Cors Fochno is where the beehives are kept. The weir is thirty yards away, situated at the bend in the Leri river that is commemorated in the present day field being marked on the tithe map of 1841 as Cae Gored (Weir Field). The Williams and Rowlands families of today's Brynllys commented on this matter by stating that they had not known about its old name, but had often wondered why there was a gravelly area arching through its corner (Williams & Rowlands, pers. comm. 2001).

The most famed legend in the Borth area is that of Cantref Gwaelod, the Lowland Hundred. It is a tale of disaster whose only survivors were later involved in the Taliesin story mentioned previously. It was they who discovered Taliesin as a foundling and gave him his name. The Cantref Gwaelod story inspired poet and essayist Thomas Love Peacock (1785-1866) who produced it in book form as *The Misfortunes of Elphin* published in 1829. No doubt he had heard the story from his Welsh connections by way of his 1819 marriage to Jane Gryffydd whom his friend Percy Bysse Shelley referred to as the 'White Snowdonian Antelope'.

The story of Cantref Gwaelod that I know is as follows:

This Cantref was held in ancient times by Gwyddno Garanhir who had his castle at Caergwyddno, situated in an area at the end of Cynfelin's causeway, which today lies under the sea ten miles off the coast. The then low lying area necessitated sea defence embankments with a watchman to guard them. Seithenin had this responsibility, which was unfortunate as he was a great drunk. Elfin, Gwyddno's son, nagged his father to no avail concerning the state of the sea defences. On a night of high tide and accompanying tempest, with Seithenin inebriated, the sea broached the dilapidated embankments and drowned forever this Lowland Hundred. All were lost except Gwyddno, Elfin and Angharad. 'Proof' of such tales is the submerged remains of a forest along Borth beach.

The Cantref Gwaelod legend was convenient to explain the remains of a sunken forest that is always visible somewhere along the Borth shoreline. Curiously, unlike other versions of this story, local tradition has not interpreted the causeways as ancient sea walls. In the Dark Ages and Medieval times the forest remains must have been more evident, to the extent that sudden inundation must have seemed the only answer to this puzzling phenomenon. According to scientific studies, there were several periods of gradual inundation triggered by rising sea levels beginning around 6000 B.C. In the Neolithic period in Britain, from 4500-2500 B.C., the human inhabitants witnessed this slow inundation which possibly continued well into the Bronze Age, 2500-800 B.C. The associated tales could have been passed down by the original pre-Celtic inhabitants of

Britain, and became mixed with the Celtic mythology, which itself had travelled across Europe and arrived in Britain about 1000 B.C. Scholarly research denies any sudden shift in land or sea levels, so obviously it was a process that lasted for centuries. It is supposed that the Romans, who recorded much of life in Britain, would have noted such events or the remains of sea walls or sunken towns (North, 1957, p.163). There have been animal remains found in the shallow seas around the Welsh coast with arrow heads amongst the bones, testifying to the fact that people had lived and hunted where the sea now is during the Mesolithic and Neolothic periods. In 1968 Mr. Aran Morris found the remains of an auroch on Borth beach. This animal, the now extinct European ox, was hunted by the ancients and its images were painted on the cave wall and ceilings at Altamira and Lascaux.

Topographic changes can be wrought by sea erosion. In some places the cliff formations between Borth and Wallog are continually changing because of rock slides. In the last thirty years even productive lobster holes, one near Craig y Delyn (Harp Cliff), and another by Carreg Mulfran (Cormorant Rock) that were accessible during the smallest of tides, have both been smashed by the sea. Another one further south opposite Carreg Felen (Yellow Rock), so named because it is covered with the lichen *xanthoria parietina*, has also been destroyed by winter gales. This was where local fisherman Aran Morris caught a record six pound lobster in 1968. The once large grass topped rock feature by Twll Ladi Wen (White Ladies Cave) near Trwyn Pellaf, that could easily be scaled forty years ago, is now no more than a large boulder. Tol Faer the folkloric contender for the weir keeper's station, situated between Wallog and Clarach, suffered the same fate centuries ago. Nowadays this submerged formation is the haunt of the lobster, the summer visitor the black bream, and in winter the cod.

Twll Ladi Wen is the site of an ancient ghost story This is the little cave where a white-draped female apparition would sometimes be seen gliding over the boulders into her cavern home. This cave has now almost disappeared as a cliff slide in the winter of 2000 saw much of it destroyed. The Reverand D.T. Hughes' articles about old Borth called *Looking Back* records this local ghost story being set further south than the one I know. Hughes' site is in the cave called Ogof y Delyn (Harp Cave), which is just north of Craig Y Delyn. His ghostly lady is not a gowned figure gliding in and out of her cave home, but a mermaid who comes ashore to comb her tresses. I began to speculate that perhaps the differing locations meant that Borth and Morfa Borth had separate versions of local stories. However Aran Morris whose antecedents have always lived at Morfa Borth, concurs that the cave is located at Trwyn Pellaf.

Ogof y Delyn is not always easy to enter, as it fills with stones after storms. Years ago when it was accessible, one entered a large round chamber with beautifully smoothed walls and a fine gravel floor. In the centre of this domed cave was a large upright stone called Carreg yr Eglwys (Church Rock). Unfortunately much of the 'ceiling' has now fallen to the floor and the solitary menhir-like 'pulpit' is no more. There are another two stories attached to this cave. It was purported to be the secret meeting place of Catholics in Tudor times. The other story is that it was the meeting place for the early Nonconformists, as they were much loathed by the established church. Prior to a law being passed in 1689, giving nonconformists the right to practice their religion, they were constantly persecuted. These stories were told by Mr Willy James, the Borth County Primary School headmaster in the 1950s. The Borth coastal strip had long evoked such stories. According to an article written about the Clarach area, concerning secret passages to and from churches:

> ... all sorts of legends were popular at one time in regard to such passages and caverns as could be seen in the rocks at Borth (Samuel, 1914, p.45).

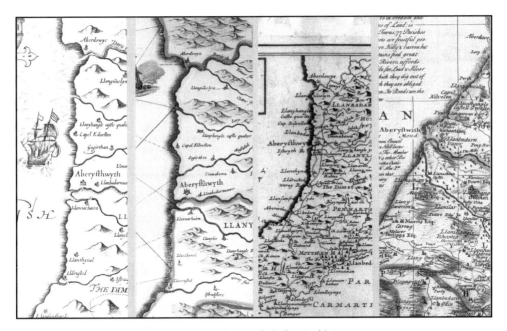

5. Maps marking Capel Kilvellen (Cynfelin)

6. Submerged forest

MAPS AND CHARTS

Of the cartographic records of the Borth area and beyond, John Speed's map of 1610 mainly denotes churches and manor houses, and overlooks scattered peasant farms. It does not mark Borth by name, but it is interesting to note that the river Leri exits well to the south. It is either a stylistic embellishment, or could support a long-held belief that the Leri once flowed into the sea near the present day lifeboat station. Folklore insisted that over the centuries the prevailing wind and tide flow from the south west had pushed the sand and shingle bank northwards and with it the river's exit. This supposition has recently been proven correct. Surveys of the beach from Trwyn Cyntaf to Ynyslas indicate that the Leri's sea exit has moved north from a position opposite today's lifeboat shed to its final exit before closure, opposite Aberleri. There are stretches of peat and clay interspersed by alluvial deposits from a waterway entering the sea at intervals all along the beach (R. A. Yates, pers. comm. 2003).

Johann Jannsen's map of the area, produced in 1650, intriguingly marks the now vanished Capel Cynfelin (Kilvellin) that stood near Clarach and was sited somewhere between the present day Wallog Mansion and Glanmor Farm. This was a religious building or settlement and is marked as such on maps dating from 1542 (Christopher Saxton) up until 1809 (John Roper). It has been suggested by Mr Alexander Jones, long time resident of Clarach, that it may very well have been a resting house, as Porthangel and Ty'r Abi were in the Cwymcynfelin area. These were places that the monks of Strata Florida Abbey stayed at on their travels northwards to the Dyfi ferry (S. Jones, pers. comm. 2003). The abbey had been given land in the Llanfihangel Genau'r Glyn area, namely Doferchen, later Tirmynach (Abbey Land). Mr Jones further conjectured that the building could have been in an area which has suffered severe erosion even in his lifetime. This is a possibility as a Saint Mary's chapel recorded in Elizabethan times at Aberystwyth was washed away in a violent storm in the 1600s. This could also have been the fate of a small rest house and chapel on the low Wallog to Clarach clifftop. Perhaps from there travellers walked under the cliff and along the beach to the Dyfi ferry, a far easier and quicker journey, tide permitting, than over the undulating coastal clifftop land route.

Lewis Morris's map of the area, made during his 1748 maritime survey *Plan of Harbours, Bars, Bays and Roads in St Georges Channel,* unfortunately excludes the Wallog to Borth strip. Many other coastal areas were not recorded, as he was mainly concerned with havens, anchorages and navigational features, especially hazards such as sandbars and causeways. The term 'barred havens' in various texts means anchorages in river-mouths "guarded" by sandbars. However the exit of the Leri is included in his chart which concentrates on the navigational features of the Dyfi estuary. That exit was opposite the present day farm/holiday resort of Aberleri. This little harbour mouth of the Leri is mentioned in Llanfihangel church records of 1728 where they state that:

> ... *ye customary tythe of herrings and of other fish from 4 fishing botes belonging and moring in Borth and Aberleri* (Bygones, 1867-8, p. 28).

Does this mean that four boats belonging to Borth moored at Aberleri, or that some were at Borth and others at the Leri mouth? Today's Aberleri farm on old Ordnance Survey maps is marked as Lower Aberleri farm, whilst a smallholding that existed somewhere near today's Borth Railway Station was called Upper Aberleri. This could have been the place that was the temporary station during the construction of the railway line to Borth and beyond in the 1860s. The land between the upper and lower Aberleri farm would therefore be referred to in the old days as Aberleri. At one time the river's exit was possibly where the Lon Goed stream met the Leri as seen in Singer's 1803 map. Today one can still clearly see the old river route as a 'rush bed' meandering through the present day golf course, especially on the north side of the house known as Glan Gors.

Borth is mentioned in the text of Lewis Morris' survey in connection with the thriving herring fishery of the early 18th century where he notes:... 'here (Aberdyfi) and at Borth they have some years a good herring fishery, and of other fish a plenty'. In his 1748 survey he was punctilious in using the local Welsh toponyms for coastal and marine features. Even though on occasion he knew how to curry favour with the English when he wanted something to his advantage, he was more often sarcastic towards them. Morris believed that the English academic establishment should, in writing about another country's history, be well versed in its language. This belief he used in his withering attacks on feeble attempts at spelling Welsh place names (Jenkins, 2002, pp.1-23).

Later surveys still resorted to convoluted Anglicised versions of place names, as in Murdoch MacKenzie's marine chart of 1775. In this chart we have a clear view of a correctly marked Borth, but with a misspelt 'Leary' river exiting at Aberleri. It is interesting to note that the then rivercourse had warranted a little bridge marked near today's Aberleri farm. If there is any significance to the number of buildings included to denote a village, then Borth and Aberdyfi were the same size. Surprisingly for 1775, there are no buildings marked on Mackenzie's chart as being part of Borth on the shingle strand; this, however may be because the space between the shoreline and the parallel course of the Leri, on this particular chart layout is too narrow to include buildings. These buildings are more about stylistic embellishment than actual house numbers as the main function of the chart is to assist mariners. Many mapmakers and also so called travellers did not in fact visit some of the areas mapped or written of, they simply used previous accounts or records.

The physical features of the Leri river mouth and its own little bar appear on several old maps and charts such as Lewis Morris's 1748 marine survey. However there are no buildings marked and it was not mentioned in the Elizabethan surveys of 1565. I speculate that there must have surely been one or two mud or stone cottages at this location as it was after all, a well-used place. Under the last few hundred yards of the shingle bank there may be the remains of old wooden constructions that mark its ancient use as a landing place. Borth fishermen used the Leri as it was conveniently tidal up to Ynys Fergi, which it still is. What may also be considered is that prior to re-routing the Leri, the volume of water entering the river system may have been greater so it could have been tidal beyond today's Glanleri/Brynllys bridge, making it easier for boats to get nearer the back of the village.

With all this in mind one wonders whether there was a settlement around the Leri sea exit when it was near today's lifeboat station, or later somewhere further north as oceandrift pushed the rivermouth in that direction. Perhaps these places were the now lost Porth Gwyddno. Considering that Gwyddno's name has been given to several features in the area, is it not possible that it was near today's Borth? Those who dismiss the idea of Porth Gwyddno being located somewhere near the village have yet to identify an alternative. It has been speculated that it was in south Scotland, possibly somewhere along the Clyde... but where? References to Porth Gwyddno being a major port may well have been poetic licence to aggrandise this location, as the alternative name, Hafan Gwyddno, can mean a home or haven. All this is surely no less plausible than Gwallawg giving his name to Wallog.

At one time the Leri and other local streams were vital in providing water for domestic use. By the end of the 19th century fresh water for Morfa Borth inhabitants was solely sourced from the Leri after the Nant y Garreg stream was diverted into the sea near today's lifeboat station. A drainage leet was dug along the back of the village to absorb the seepage from the marshland and several small streams, one of which passed through Felin Wern and another that flowed down Cwmcethin. In old deeds this leet is called the Old Mill Leet (J. Matthews, pers. comm. 2003). This was mockingly called *Yr Afon Sain,* the River Seine. To gather water the womenfolk would walk down the Rhyd to the river Leri and fill their jugs or pails every morning. There was consternation at Evelwen in the 1870s when one of the young daughters of John Beynon set her petticoat alight when she stood too near the peat fire. A whole days supply of water was swiftly thrown over her to prevent a serious burn. As it was towards evening propriety deemed that it was the menfolk who returned to the Leri to replenish the water (J.Richards, pers. comm. 1970). Water for the upper Borth and Gwastad area was plentiful with sources at Nant y Garreg, Nant y Wennol and the many springs in the area.

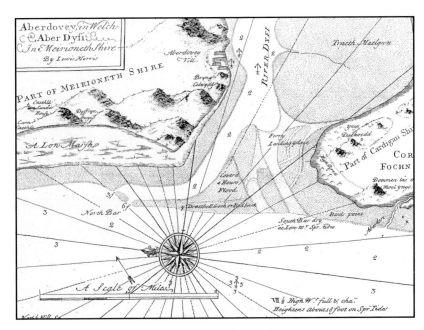

7. Lewis Morris's chart, 1748

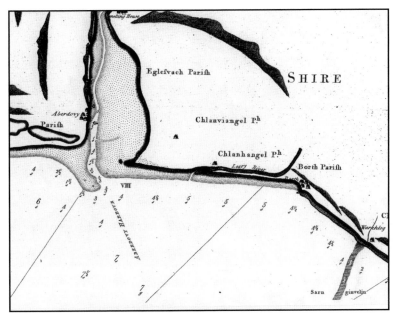

8. Murdock Mackenzie's chart, circa 1775

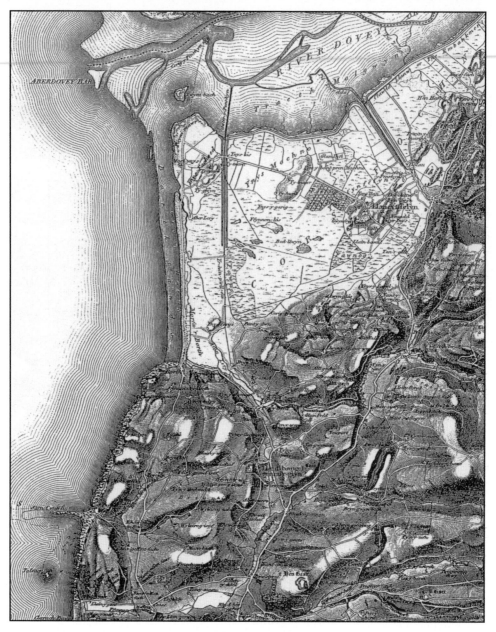

9. Segment of Ordinance Survey map, 1841

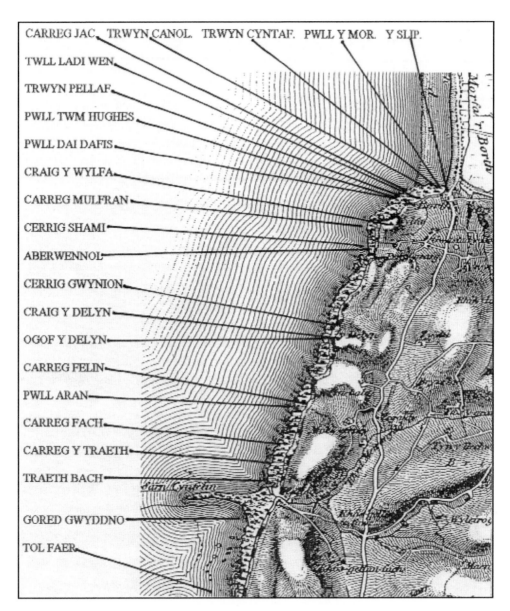

CARREG JAC. TRWYN CANOL. TRWYN CYNTAF. PWLL Y MOR. Y SLIP.

TWLL LADI WEN

TRWYN PELLAF

PWLL TWM HUGHES

PWLL DAI DAFIS

CRAIG Y WYLFA

CARREG MULFRAN

CERRIG SHAMI

ABERWENNOL

CERRIG GWYNION

CRAIG Y DELYN

OGOF Y DELYN

CARREG FELIN

PWLL ARAN

CARREG FACH

CARREG Y TRAETH

TRAETH BACH

GORED GWYDDNO

TOL FAER

10. Toponyms between Borth and Wallog

31

THE YNYSLAS AREA

This area is redolent with ghosts as it was here that the Borth crew of the *Venus*, a small sloop, lost their lives, save only for the captain. Recently a few wrecks just opposite the old Leri mouth have been discovered, amongst which could be the *Venus*. This location must have been hazardous as not only did the Leri have a small sandbar, but nearby was the large and potentially more dangerous one at the Dyfi river entrance. It was here at the Dyfi mouth that disaster struck on a February night in 1839. A ship's boat taking a party of four young ladies and three crew members out to the anchored brigantine *Favorite* missed the vessel in the dark and the ferocious ebb took them to their doom on the Dyfi Bar. Of the seven drowned the bodies of able seaman, John Angel of Aberdyfi and the young ships apprectice, Lewis of Tywyn, were found on the beach between Moelynys and Borth.

It was not only ships and their crews that were lost offshore in this vicinity. The following tale adds to its sinister reputation. It was somewhere on the seaward side of the dunes opposite Moelynys that a Barmouth doctor disappeared in the early 19th century (Morgan, 1948, p.79). Having crossed the estuary by ferry he disembarked with the rest of the passengers on the south side to make for the inn at Moelynys guided by marker poles driven into the sandflats. However, the doctor wandered off, never to be seen again. A search on the following day revealed his neatly stacked pile of clothes near the edge of the sea. It was reported as being misadventure through swimming but there was speculation that it may have been suicide. The previously mentioned marker poles can be seen in an 1840 etching of the Dyfi Estuary that appears in W.D. Morgan's *Brief Glory*. Another illustration in the same book depicts sheep being herded into the ferryboat on the Borth side of the estuary.

On the maps of the 18th and 19th century Twyni Mawr (Large Dunes), and Twyni Bach (Small Dunes), at Ynyslas, are marked as being quite separate with a substantial beach area between them, which does not exist today. This suggests that at an earlier time there were no Twyni Bach, and that Traeth Maelgwn was a much bigger beach. Traeth Maelgwn is the strip of beach running from the sea edge up the estuary alongside the Dyfi river to the Clettwr stream. It is named after the Welsh king who died of the plague in 547 and was buried in Llandrillo-yn- Rhos, near Llandudno. It was on this beach that the kingship of North Wales was once decided, so an ancient tale tells us. This is the version I know:

On the Borth side of the Dyfi estuary there is a beach known as Traeth Maelgwn. It was named after Maelgwn Gwynedd who was elected King at this site around A.D. 500. At this time efforts were being made to unite the Britons against the incursions of the Angles, Saxons and sea Vikings. Maelgwn had already become famous for defending Anglesey against the Vikings and he was known as the Island Dragon. He marched southwards determined to unite the warring princes of Wales under his leadership. The meeting place was the mouth of the Dyfi estuary on the south side along the sea-front and into the estuary itself. All the princes had their entourage of courtiers and advisers. Maelgwn's chief advisor was Maeldaf who was descended from the Princes of the sons of Coel who refused ever to be English. Maeldaf knew the tidal idiosyncrasies of the Dyfi well and used this knowledge to his master's advantage. No doubt the election of the king was settled by the sword with the opposition thwarted or drowned by their ignorance of the swift tidal flow whose treacherous path they had been manoeuvred into by Maeldaf. Tradition has it that Maeldaf built a chair for his master that floated on a raft of waxed feathers gathered from a nearby bird roosting rock, still known to this day as Craig y Deryn, (Bird Rock). Folklore states that the person appointed king would be the one who remained seated last. This device saw the king float safely amidst all the disarray... thus Maelgwn was duly elected and the event was commemorated in the beach name.

From this beach at the dunes' end one has a clear view of Aberdyfi. Only about three hundred yards of water at low ebb divides the two shores, but what a division of time and memory between the peoples of Borth and Aberdyfi. In the 19th century it was a busy route, with mariners travelling backwards and forwards between the two places. Up until half a century ago there was a metal tower that one stood on to wave to the ferryman near Cerrig y Penrhyn... nowadays there is no ferry.

Eastwards up the estuary lie the vast cockle grounds that would have been more accessible for the cockling and shrimping ladies of the early 19th century since the then non-existent Leri river did not provide the barrier that it does today. There was only a slight seepage stream called Pil yr Ynys. Today, there is a boat building yard just below the road bridge across the Leri. This is in a sense a resurrection as there was a small ship yard here from the middle of the 19th century. To the north of the boatyard there is a good cockle ground, often marked by the appearance from under the sand of the ribs of three unidentified old sloops that were sunk there to form a revetment. This was to prevent the re-routed Leri river flow from silting. It is a sad end and a pathetic monument to a glorious era; but the one consolation is that these vessels are buried in their home region within a mile or so of where they were creatively and skilfully constructed.

This makes one ponder on what the village fishermen thought of the landowners who diverted the course of the Leri into the Dyfi, thus depriving them of a convenient coastal access. Working under the General Enclosure Act of 1801, local land owners diverted the Leri by cutting a channel northwards from Ynys Dwrgi (Otter Island) to Ynyslas where the river now entered the estuary and not the sea. The idea was to create new farms from the reclaimed lands so that they could be rented out. There was an ever increasing demand for new farmland as the rural, as well as the industrial population of Wales began to expand. The project began when the prime movers the Pryses of Gogerddan and Matthew Davies of Cwmcynfelin received royal assent in 1813. The whole project took nearly 34 years to complete as legal and monetary issues were not settled until 1847. As to the matter of any local dissent, R.J. Colyer the author of a paper entitled *The enclosure and drainage of Cors Fochno (Borth bog) 1813-1847*, had not found any documented evidence of protest. He was not surprised however since the local land owners did not consult the peasantry in decision making or record localised dissent. But there was a kind of people's justice system within communities. It was expected at the time that the local community would maintain the diverted Leri and other drainage systems. Colyer noted that this had not happened; therefore it can be conjectured that there may have been some protest against the river diversion (R.J. Colyer, pers. comm. 2001).

However, it would have been only the small boat owners who could have accessed the old Leri sea exit. The more ambitious may have seen the new Leri mouth as ideal for shipbuilding within a sheltered estuary near the expanding port of Aberdyfi. The maritime future lay more with international trading than fishing or coastal trade as far as Borth was concerned, considering its limiting location on an open beach. It is interesting to note that D. W. Morgan, a native of Aberdyfi but of Borth descent, did not know that the Leri had previously flowed into the sea (Morgan, 1948, p.24). From about 1830 those fishermen who had used the Leri mouth had no option but to launch their boats from an open beach or move to a more convenient harbour such as Aberystwyth.

SHIPPING DEVELOPMENT

From about 1600 onwards the increase in Ceredigion's population and wealth meant a growing demand for consumer goods, the majority of which had to come by sea. This boosted the need for ships, men to sail them and the development of ancilliary service industries such as rope and sail-making. An important factor in all this was King George III's Shipping Act of 1786, instituted for the further increase and promotion of shipping and navigation, whereby the value of every ship was divided into 64 parts, encouraging small capital investors. A unit of ownership was called 'an ounce' and consisted of four shares, which were sometimes sold or bequeathed in parts. This meant that a vessel's ownership could became quite complex. This share division was based on the fact that there were 16 ounces to the pound, therefore, four times sixteen equalled the 64 parts of a ship. This new dynamic had a positive impact on small communities such as Borth as it allowed business enterprise to flourish in poor areas. It was also one of the few opportunities that tenant farmers in the region could have for private investment and the shipping records show that they did just that.

The establishment of Friendly Societies at the beginning of the 19th century was another way in which local people could work together for their mutual benefit. One such society, the Order of Ivorites, was formed in Wrexham by Thomas Robert Jones of Llannefydd, in 1836. In 1841 the Castell Gwallter Ivorite Lodge was established in Llandre (Owens, 1956, p.25). Each member contributed a monthly subscription that went into a benefit fund for the members and their families. It was in essence a much needed health and social benefit system. The subscription money was invested in mortgages, to purchase property and occasionally vessels. The Ivorites' account books held in the National Library Aberystwyth, reveal that many farmers and blacksmiths from the Borth area were subscribers, as were some ninety mariners. One can trace the involvement of Borth Captain, John Simon, from his initial subscription through to his death. He owned the sloop *Robust*, built in Aberarth in 1797, which he bought in 1832, and had her re-registered at Aberystwyth in that same year. He died in March 1881 at 74 years of age.

Borth's Captain Thomas Davies financed the purchase of his schooner *Nathaniel* in 1879 with the help of a £360 loan from the Ivorites. This 110 ton vessel was bought from Porthmadoc owners and had been built at Caernarvon in 1868 by William Griffith. Earlier, another Thomas Davies, associated with the *Venus*, had been assisted in buying the sloop *Endeavour*. One interesting entry notes that Captain John Lewis of Borth, who had previously not asked for anything from the society was forced by circumstances to seek financial help as his schooner Ocean had been wrecked in Cornish waters. Another entry indicates that some members were not so enchanted with life at sea, and a Shadrack Morris was listed initially as a mariner, but later as a carrier and then a miller.

The Ivorite records show that there were two vessels named *Friendship* both owned and operated by two Borth brothers. The larger and older of the two Friendships weighing 45 tons was built at Llugwy in the Dyfi estuary in 1788 and traded for at least 60 years. The smaller 17 ton vessel was built at Aberarth in 1826, and was affectionately known locally, and noted in the Ivorite papers, as *Y Friendship Fach*, the Little Friendship. William Jones was the principal skipper of this vessel, whilst at other times John Arter and the two sloops' owners, the brothers John and Evan Hughes took command. The small sloop foundered in a squall off a location that is difficult to read in the Aberystwyth Shipping Register. It looks like Pygyn Point, so it may be Pen Pygyn. These vessels are commemorated in the name of the old Borth pub, the Friendship Inn. One of the last of the Hughes' associated with the inn and sloops was David Hughes who died in 1904 aged 80. His wife Martha had predeceased him in 1893 aged 62.

In 1786, the Statutory Registers of Shipping were introduced and Aberystwyth took over as the main port from Aberdyfi; it also gained a custom house. Aberdyfi henceforth becomes a sub-port. Despite this new responsibility, Aberystwyth still tarried until 1840 in making improvements to its harbour. Although for centuries an important fishing centre, the harbour was too shallow for larger vessels. This was largely due to its continual silting caused by longshore drift and tidal activity. Up until that year, imported timber from North America was brought to Aberdyfi by Aberystwyth vessels, such as the *Hero* and the brig *Credo*. Their cargoes were then floated in huge rafts southward past Borth to the ships home port (Lloyd, 1998, p80). Such complications finally spurred improvements at Aberystwyth harbour.

Even as the demand for larger ships grew, local shipwrights still built on the same sites and under the same conditions as they had for sloops. These shipbuilders seldom worked from detailed plans, but taking their own initiative, intuitively and skilfully constructed not only sturdy coastal vessels but some of the finest schooners built anywhere. The schooner had evolved..."from the apple dumpling design she developed in the course of 25 years into a longer, leaner and more beautiful ship altogether "(Morgan, 1949, p. 109). Usually a half hull wooden model was made in consultation with the prospective owners' needs. Aberdyfi's ablest shipbuilder, Thomas Richards, built the *Dovey Belle* and the *Lizzie Jane* for Borth owners. Another Aberdyfi man, John Jones, built the following schooners for Borth skippers, *Jane and Mary, Beatrice, Sarah,* and the *Sarah Davies*. This shipbuilder was driven to distraction by the Borth owners' fastidious insistence that quality and care should be invested in their purchases, so much so that in a drunken fit he cursed them and demanded that upon his death he be buried well away from them. Prospective captains of new ships often supervised the building, which seems reasonable when one considers that their lives depended on the quality of materials and workmanship involved.

After the Leri was diverted into the Dyfi estuary shipbuilding took place at the Lerry Bridge yard, whose main customers were Borth residents. Built there were the sloops *Mary and Ellen* 1842, *Mary Rees* 1842, *Claudia* 1850, *Priscilla* 1855; the brigantine *Island Maid* 1851; the schooners *Gleanor* 1849, *Resolute* 1849 and the smack Catherine 1864. To date the only ship recorded as having been built on the Borth foreshore somewhere opposite todays Railway Inn, was the schooner *Catherine & Ellen* in 1842. This schooner's construction seems a large enterprise to have been the first foray into shipbuilding undertaken at this location. One wonders whether any smaller type of vessels had been built there previously. The local type of fishing boat certainly would have been before its design was taken to Aberystwyth around 1840. If the dates for the first Lerry Bridge yard vessel launchings are correct, then from 1842 onwards the Ynyslas location was recognised as being far more convenient for shipbuilding than the trickier Borth foreshore.

Every small port in Ceredigion seems to lay claim to having provided the sea transportation for the first organ to St David's cathedral. Borth's contender is the previously mentioned schooner *Catherine and Ellen*; David Hughes the younger, being master and owner. On her launching in 1842 she was blessed by the Rev. John Jones of Glanleri Farm. This is the John Jones who was courted so assiduously by the vicar of Llandre who even offered him a curacy in the parish if he would take up a teaching post under the auspices of the church. However, he was not dissuaded from his staunch Calvinistic Methodist leanings (Enoch, 2002, p.53). Earlier, Glanleri Farm had provided the Llanfihangel Genau'r Glyn church with a vicar called John Gwynne in the 1700s.

In *Brief Glory* D.W. Morgan supplies the reader with the complete costings of the construction of two Dyfi built schooners. The *Mary and Ellen* built in 1872 by Thomas Richards cost a total of £1,832/5/2. An ounce, four shares, of this ship was worth approximately £114, still a lot of money for most... no wonder even a share, in this case £28, was often divided amongst family members in Borth. The *Jane Gwynne* built in 1858 by John Jones cost altogether, including sundries, £1,585/1/1. An ounce share in this vessel was approximately £98 (Morgan, 1948, pp.120-122 & pp.130-132). According to Lewis Lloyd, sloops were also expensive to build when one considers that the Amity built at Derwenlas, cost nearly £1,000 (Lloyd, 1996, p.155). This seems an incredible sum of money for 1802. A Newquay sloop of 54 tons, the *Catherine,* built by John Evans in 1829, cost £822/12/0 (Campbell-Jones, 1975, p.281).

In the latter half of the 19th century the increasing demand for schooners of 80-120 tons, saw that vessel overtaking the larger, square-rigged ships as a favoured vessel as they were easier to handle when sailing in and out of the small ports of Ceredigion. The schooner was also responsible for bringing about the demise of the existing fleet of coastal trading sloops which had evolved over the preceeding centuries to suit local conditions. This expansion in schooner building was spurred by the slate exporting boom in west Wales that coincided with the region's final involvement with merchant sailing ships. Many of these locally built schooners travelled far afield in search of cargoes. They went to Europe, the Mediterranean, the West Indies and to Newfoundland and back across the north Atlantic. Of the local schooner fleet the last two built at Aberdyfi were the *Sabrina* in 1879 and the *Olive Branch* in 1880. The former had Borth connections with Sabrina Cottage.

The square-rigged barques and brigantines of Aberdyfi and other local ports sailed to the Far East and also around Cape Horn to such ports as Iquique and Valparaiso. The barque *Caradog* whose captain was a Borth master mariner, Lewis Williams was the largest sailing ship registered at Aberystwyth. Most of these local vessels could not enter their home ports and therefore traded from harbours which were more accessible than those on the Ceredigion seaboard. Local ownership of these larger and increasingly estranged vessels declined swiftly. This resulted in a number of Borth masters being employed to command ships owned by companies based at deep water ports elsewhere. Large sailing vessels, such as the Liverpool barque *Rose Hill,* commanded by Borth's Evan Jenkins, were a last ditch attempt to challenge the increasing supremacy of steam toward the end of the 19th century.

The barque *Glendovey* (not to be confused with the smaller Canadian built barque also named *Glendovey,* owned by Machynlleth merchants, which often bought timber cargoes to the Dyfi), was a 588 ton vessel and was the largest sailing ship whose home port was Aberdyfi. Built at Sunderland in 1876 by James Laing at the Deptford yard, it was owned by William James of Borth, and fellow villagers had shares in her. This vessel was captained by John Williams also of Borth, who sailed her all over the world from 1876 to 1900. Captain Williams took command when he was 40 years of age and continued until his retirement at 64 years of age. This ship sailed to both coasts of South America and undertook the arduous Cape Horn passage on her way to Chile and Peru. Other than local Welshmen employed as 1st and 2nd mates, the crew consisted mainly of German, Norwegian, Finnish and Swedish seamen employed from the *Glendovey's* stops at north European ports. Below is a brief list of the *Glendovey's* voyages from 1876 to 1898 compiled from Lewis Lloyd's account of this vessel's working life (Lloyd, 1998, pp.213-17).

1876. Sunderland-Monte Video-London
1877. London - Cape Town - Rangoon - London
1879. London - Wellington - Valparaiso - Fulcahuano - Hull
1880. Tyne - Iquique - Glasgow
1881. Glasgow - Valparaiso - Dunkirk - Swansea

1882. Swansea - Antofagasta - Carrezal - Boya - Iquique - Hamburg

1883. Hamburg - Iquique - Cardiff

1885. Glasgow - Valparaiso - Hamburg

1887. Antwerp - Valparaiso - London

1890. Liverpool - Callao - Dunkirk - Liverpool

1891. Liverpool - Iquiquie - Rotterdam - Cardiff

1892. Cardiff - Iquique - Antwerp

1893. Antwerp - Barry - River Plate - Sharpness

1894. Sharpness - Cardiff - River Plate - Cardiff

1895. Liverpool - Buenos Aires - Cardiff

1896. Cardiff - Rosaria - Cardiff

1896. Cardiff - River Plate - Newcastle-On-Tyne

1897. Newcastle-On-Tyne - Rosario - Liverpool

1898. Liverpool - Rosario - Barry - Hamburg – Preston

This barque carried a total compliment of twelve crew members and her trading scope was wide, enabling her to voyage to any port within the limits of 60 degrees north and 60 degrees south. Some Borth men who served on the *Glendovey* were Morgan Jones, John H. Roberts and John Jones as 1st mates, and Llewelyn Rees and John Davies as 2nd mates.

The *Glendovey's* records show that there were a few desertions amongst the crew at various ports, such as Rosario and Valpariso. As with many other Welsh ships it was 'dry', meaning no alcohol, so maybe the temptations of these exotic ports proved too much for some, as attested by the fact that several crew members contracted venereal diseases. On one voyage in 1876 the twenty eight year old 1st mate Thomas Walters of New Quay, had to leave the ship in Valpariso to have a severe abscess treated, but he soon rejoined the vessel at Pisaqua. This New Quay man went on to become a master mariner and in that capacity often employed Borth men, some of whom he is seen with in the crew photograph of the *S.S. Glanhafren* taken in 1894.

In Ceredigion, from the middle of the 19th century everything maritime was gravitating towards a world-wide trading format that necessitated greater skills, such as more sophisticated navigational knowledge. It has been noted that navigational instruction was very late in arriving in Aberdyfi, with a Captain Walter beginning classes in 1880 (Lloyd, 1998, p.165). Borth men were better served as, with so many master mariners in families, skills were handed down from father to son. There were also informal navigational classes conducted at private houses, of which there were two in Borth. One was at Tymawr run by Captain John Jones who levied a fee of threepence a week for tuition, the other was at today's Harlequin Café, on the site where an old cottage called Noddfa once stood sideways to the road. Miss Rees of Arequipa, daughter of Captain Dafydd Rees, called it a nautical school. Captain Rees who owned several vessels, was born in Sabrina cottage, as was his father before him, another Captain Dafydd Rees (Stan Evans, pers. comm. 2003).

Some remarkable women taught navigation in Wales. In tiny Llangrannog, Ceredigion, there lived the extremely gifted Sarah Jane Rees, or to give her Bardic name 'Cranogwen' (1839-1916). Rees imparted her knowledge, via her navigational classes, to the local maritime aspirants. According to Susan Campbell-Jones, there was also a woman navigation teacher at Aberystwyth. (Campbell-Jones, 1975, p.296). In Caernarfonshire, Mrs Ellen Edwards (1810-1889), another daughter of a master mariner, taught navigational skills to generations of seamen in her 60-year career. Intriguingly, in one of the photographs of Borth's skippers a woman has been given central place in the composition. I speculate that this hitherto unknown woman may have taught navigation to Borth skippers as well as English, so that class members could gain this much needed linguistic skill. An aspiring officer would need this knowledge to understand the questions likely to be asked in master mariner examinations, and later in the keeping of logbooks. Years ago I viewed one of Captain William Richards' diaries and his entries are very much a Welshman's version of English, as in bort two sospans, meaning... bought two saucepans.

As previously stated, Borth's maritime role is not only subsumed under the history of Aberdyfi, but visual evidence of this era, still so prevalent in the 1940s and 50s is fading rapidly. There are hardly any artefacts left of this maritime past. In my childhood, every home had a painted sailing ship with family associations on their walls, yet today I know of only a few paintings of Borth vessels in the village. These ship paintings were icons of a family's success, therefore there was social cachet attached to them. In a sense they were the equivalent of the symbolic paintings of prize animals by prosperous farmers. Many of these ships paintings were commissioned on the spot from what were known as pierhead artists. Most of them worked on a canvas that already contained a painted-in sea and sky ready to include whatever ship was going to be depicted. Some had pre-painted local features such as harbour entrances, lighthouses or Mount Vesuvius if the ship was in the vicinity of Naples. Some paintings, although charming, have a static ambience as they feature vessels with wind filled sails on an improbably calm sea with pendants and flags streaming defiantly into the wind!

The images of the *Charlotte* and the *Catherine Morgan* are depicted at the same location since the backgrounds are identical; probably by the same artist. Another painting of the *Charlotte* by L. Renault, shows her entering Leghorn. In this work, as well as the slight change in the sail pattern he has included a personal touch in the left hand corner, where one of the background vessels is actually the *Charlotte* leaving Leghorn. Perhaps the slight change in rig had something to do with the change of master as Borth skipper Richard Jones was in command for four years whilst previously Thomas Daniel of Aberdyfi had been in charge. More knowing artists have depicted the *Pluvier* and the *Nerissa* as they demonstrate an understanding of seagoing reality. In both these paintings the sail distribution is in accord with the stormy seas as the square sails are down and the main sails partly reefed. Another knowledgeable, but unknown painter, depicts the barque *Drusus* champing at the bit at the beginning of her voyage. A pilot boat has just left her outside an unknown Welsh port. Could it be Aberdyfi, as Captain David Rees of Borth owned and commanded this vessel in the 1880s?

Borth mariners certainly continued and expanded their role beyond the port of Aberdyfi after its decline. The following statement makes it clear that they were Aberdyfi's life blood in its heyday as a port. Apparently after their withdrawal from Aberdyfi's maritime role, Merionethshire's local contribution faded noticeably:

On the available evidence it does seem that the seafaring propensity of the men of Borth remained throughout World War 1, markedly greater than that of the men of Aberdyfi and south Merioneth generally... besides, as has been seen, Borth was the major source of seamen for Aberdyfi during the most successful years of the port. The strength of the seafaring tradition at Borth was surely a major factor (Lloyd, L., 1998, p 265).

CARGOES

The shipping activity on the Dyfi no doubt magnetised the subsistence fishermen of Borth into seeking employment and commercial opportunity there since by the end of the 18th century Borth mariners began to run and eventually purchase their own vessels. In their first concerted effort into shipping, sloops were preferred because they were ideal for coastal trading around the Irish sea. Borth was an extremely poor village, and shares in vessels would be owned by many people other than the one person listed. This arrangement meant that vessels were often owned by one large and extended family, especially as previously mentioned, even small sloops could be expensive to purchase.

Metal ores were an important commodity that helped accelarate the expansion of the north Ceredigion shipping industry. It is thought that the Romans first exploited the County's metal resources. In the 1976 drought the remains of a Roman fort was discovered near the Llangynfelin church site. Abandoned in A.D.130 it could have been located there to exploit the nearby lead and silver deposits (Breverton, 2000, pp.170-1).

By the 1600s the lead and silver mines of north Ceredigion were yielding enormous profits. No wonder the Ysgair Hir mine and others in the area are marked on John Carey's map as the *Welch Potosi*. Sir Hugh Middleton owned one mine that produced £2000 worth of ore a month for quite a number of years. Much of these profits went to support the Royalist cause, and local silver ore was minted into coins at Aberystwyth Castle for the same cause. This activity eventually caused the parliamentary forces to reduce the fortification to ruins. The enormous potential of Ceredigion's mines to generate wealth 300 years ago is evident in the following:

> Mr Waller, Captain of the Mines under Sir Carberry Pryse, writes in 1693, that by employing 600 miners, loading at Glandyfi- a creek of Aberdyf — thence by river boats to the 'big storehouse at Aberdyfi', it was possible to export via Aberdovey 15,000 tons of lead ore, or 10,000 tons of lead, to the value of £90,000 annually (Thomas, 1946, p.46).

In the 1700's the multi-talented Lewis Morris of Anglesey arrived in Ceredigion to become involved with the lead industry. He used his engineering skills to improve mining practices and upgrade transportation systems. Morris played an important role in the county's maritime legacy with his journals and maps, which were essentially to facilitate the safer shipping of the valuable lead export. It was a considerable achievement to persuade the naval authorities to employ him as a marine surveyor and underwrite a coastal survey of Wales. This was no doubt helped by the fact that his brother Richard worked at the Admiralty.

The majority of the local land-owning gentry invested very little of their own money in venture capital. In mining, they only sold the mineral rights to prospective investors. Surprisingly, none of the gentry invested in shipping. At times there was much rivalry between the landowners, especially as some mines were very lucrative. In 1751, landowner Thomas Powell of Nanteos, claiming lord of the Manorship of Aberystwyth, tried to levy a toll on the lead ore of Gogerddan Estate owner Thomas Pryse, which had to be exported from the port. During this short-lived, avarice-driven blockade, an attempt was made by Pryse to ship Cwmsymlog's lead ore from Clarach Bay.

Not only was lead mining profitable at some workings, its fiscal potential should be considered in the context of the fact that nearly a third of all Britain's lead production came from Wales. Not only did shipping benefit from mining endeavours road systems were also developed so that pack horses and cart trains could carry the ore down to the creeks and harbours for export to England and Europe. In 1753 Lewis Morris had to build a road to transport the ore from the Esgair Mine. As was the case for other commercial products, sea routes were the cheapest and often the only feasible form of transport up to the 1860s. At one time copper mined from the Merionethshire side of the Dyfi was also an export cargo, and in the years between 1791 and 1794 a total of 1,124 tons of copper ore left via the port of Aberdyfi (Thomas, 1946, p.9).

The environmental price paid for mining the metals was substantial. A fisherman called John Jones from Aberystwyth, stated that lead pollution from the rivers Rheidol and Ystwyth had poisoned the herring spawning grounds in the area from the 1840's onwards. This was recorded by Frank Buckland and Spencer Walpole, who interviewed fishermen at Aberystwyth in 1878 whilst compiling the *Report of the Sea Fisheries Of England and Wales*. By the beginning of the 20th century the Ystwyth and Rheidol rivers were polluted to such a degree that they were described as fishless sewers:

> ... used almost solely for the lawless and selfish benefit of industries which could well afford to take proper means to effectively prevent the poisoning of the waters... there must be something radically wrong in the administration of the pollution laws (Grimble, 1913, p.162)

Oak timber products of varying kinds including beams, planks, props and bark were another major export from the Dyfi valley area, so much so that its woodlands became seriously depleted. Oak bark was exported to Ireland in astounding quantities up until the 1890s. The Rev. Walter Davies in his agricultural surveys of Wales in 1810 and 1815, noted this, and riled against what he considered, even in those days, to be environmental malpractices (Davies, 1810, p.249 & Davies, 1815, pp.19-20). There had been other dissenting voices in the past objecting to the ravaging of Welsh woodlands, such as an anonymous 16th century Welsh poet who lamented the destructive practices of charcoal burning in his poem 'Coed Glyn Cynon' (Glyn Cynon Wood), (Parry, 1962, P.550).

In the 18th century salt was such an expensive commodity that it became a prime item on the smugglers' agenda. The duties it attracted made it difficult for the poor to access this product that was so essential in preserving the meat and fish that sustained them over the winter months. No wonder many places along the Ceredigion coastline became engaged in illegal activities out of sheer necessity. In 1704 customs officers were set upon with sticks and stones by a large gathering of local people who were caught unloading this contraband from Ireland on beaches near Newquay, in South Ceredigion (Davies, 1936. p.312). There were no salt duties in Ireland and it was a third of the price charged on mainland Britain. Such was the importance of salt that earlier, in 1567, a salt-works was set up in the Dyfi estuary by speculators, but unfortunately there is no mention of how it fared. Its very existence is only noted through old shipping records. Listed in the Port Books of Aberdyfi is the record of a French carrack sailing into the Dyfi during this salt work enterprise, with a speculative cargo consisting of 15 tons of salt, of all things, and 5 tons of wine. D. W. Morgan conjectures that the salt-work operators would surely have been somewhat taken aback. However, the wine may have greased the wheels of commerce, as 18 days later *Le Seahog de Emdin* departed with 15 tons of lead ore; having successfully sold the salt and wine. The ships that brought salt cargoes to Ceredigion ports often left with barrelled herrings and oak bark (Morgan, 1948, pp. 9-11).

Activity in Ceredigion coastal shipping was further boosted in the second half of the 18th century with the increasing use of lime to neutralise the acidic soils of the county. To service this industry more locally built vessels were needed, and sloops were ideal. These oak built vessels had to be sturdily constructed as the pressure of heavy cargoes was substantial on their hulls, especially when left high and dry on beaches and river banks by an ebbing tide. Carts were drawn alongside the beached sloops in some places so that the cargoes could be swiftly unloaded before the returning tide. They were so well built that some like the *Seven Brothers*, one of the last sloops out of Derwenlas before its closure as a port in 1863, was converted into a schooner to be captained by James Morgan of Borth in the 1870s. Another consideration in their design was the necessity for a shallow draught, to facilitate the navigation of small, narrow rivers and inlets that they had to manoeuvre. Vessels for the lime trade were built on convenient riverbanks and beaches on the county's seaboard. It was in these coastal 'workhorse' vessels that generations of seafarers learned their trade, plying a shallow coastline with few sheltered harbours that were often difficult to access. There were many navigational hazards such as causeways and treacherous sandbars jealously guarding the havens of Cardigan, Aberystwyth, Aberdyfi and, possibly, Borth when the Leri flowed into the sea.

The coastal limestone carriers were usually crewed by three men. Often the sloops and the kilns were part owned by farmers. This meant that they had some semblance of control as the vagaries of agriculture could be harsh. Using lime to boost the poor soils of the area helped to ensure a supply of corn for bread-making. In the Elizabethan period, to alleviate famine, grain had been traded to the central Welsh coastal area from the more fortunate areas of Pembrokeshire on such vessels as *Le Mary Fortune, George, Sonday, Angell* and the *Le Jesus.* (Morgan, 1948, p.18). Later Oliver Cromwell sent a famine relief ship to the Dyfi area to avert one catastrophe. A certain London merchant, Luke Lucy, pleaded with the dictator's Privy Council to send a corn cargo to Aberdyfi. The Council responded favourably and sent the *John of Middleburgh* under convoy to the Dyfi escorted by the naval ship *Happy Entrance* commanded by Captain Badiley (Morgan. 1948, p 20). Borth was no doubt one of the many places in the area that suffered such travails and emphasises the importance of the seasonal herring bounty.

Limestone, and often the coal and culm (coal dust or anthracite gathered into balls held together with clay) to fire the kilns were bought in from Caernarfonshire, Pembrokeshire and Carmarthenshire to the many coastal and estuarine kiln sites, such as those at Borth. Coal and culm for domestic and light industry needs were also regular cargoes brought to the county. Culm carried by Captain Thomas Davies of Borth in the sloop *Venus* in 1828 cost 12 shillings a ton (Morgan, 1948, p.198). At the height of this trade there was a whole rash of limekilns along the Ceredigion coastline. It must have been quite a sight to see these kilns being fired, especially at night. Depending on the size of the kiln, the firing process could take many days. As well as a continuously stoked fire at the base of the kiln, alternate layers of culm and limestone ensured that the entire load was burnt. The lime for the most part still held its shape, and in this state was called lump lime. It and any powdered lime was transported by cart to the fields. This could be a tricky business as it was still very hot and the carts were made of wood. It was usually scattered over the field and left to weather and when eventually it turned into powder it was ploughed into the earth. Occasionally the lump lime was placed in a kind of bed on the side of the field and covered with soil to weather, later to be spread on the land.

There are numerous recollections concerning the lime kilns that stood on the foreshore at Borth in the late 18th and early 19th century. They were part of the once plentiful kilns on the Ceredigion coastline which were to become redundant by the 1870s. Jac Richards, stated that his grandmother, Mrs Beynon daughter of Evan Griffiths the local carpenter, spoke of two lime kilns (J. Richards, pers. comm. 2000). The previously mentioned recollections of Reverend D.T. Hughes, record that there were three lime kilns on the Borth foreshore. No doubt there was more than one of these kilns near the present lifeboat station. Under the road outside today's Spar shop, workers constructing the first sewage system in Borth in the 1960s discovered parts of a stone built wall and an arch which were probably the remains of one of the kilns. Verification of the existence and location of Borth lime kilns comes from the 1841 tithe lists. As a guide to the divisions of the townships in which Borth lies, the charts quite clearly indicate that where the Glanwern road intersects Borth's main road there was a lime kiln and that to the north lay the township of Henllys and to the south that of Cyfoeth y Brenin.

The Welsh word for kiln is odyn, and in Borth we have a farm called Brynrodyn, now a caravan park, inland from Aberwennol. I have scoured the records in vain to see if there was a kiln site on this farm or down on the beach at Aberwennol. This would have been an ideal lime landing place, and perhaps an old kiln on the foreshore there may have long since vanished. Another possibility is that there was an intermittent or field kiln somewhere on the farm indicating it was only a temporary structure. This still meant that limestone had to be shipped to the site. To add further confusion the word odyn also referred to corn drying kilns.

Limekilns had to be sufficiently robust to withstand the weather and the lumps of limestone thrown into them. The Wallog kiln, built of stones from the shoreline has, like others that dot the Ceredigion coastline, recently been renovated to its original state. This kiln south of Borth, was apparently only fired a few times. There was a complex series of roadways and gateways organised in readiness for facilitating the deployment of lime to the local farms inland as far as Ruel Farm. Traces of these scarcely used 'lanes' can still be seen today (I. Mason, pers comm. 2000). As with other transportable commodities it was the arrival of the railways that heralded the decline of the maritime lime trade. Curiously in 1779, there was a smelting house at Wallog which had to be abandoned after a year as the boat loads of coal from Aberystwyth to fuel its activities were prevented from depositing their cargoes because of the persistent ground swell there. One wonders if this situation also affected the use of the nearby lime kiln.

An artist known as the 'Aberystwyth Primitive' has left us an insight into the hazards of the lime and culm trade in the first half of the 19th century in the Aberystwyth area. One of this artist's works depicts the wrecking of a Borth vessel. The *John and Mary*, a 44 ton sloop built at Lerry Bridge in 1842, got into trouble whilst bringing culm from South Wales to Aberdyfi. The vessel was named after the captain, Evan Hughes's parents. On the 9th of February, 1848, whilst approaching Aberdyfi in heavy seas, her steering gear was damaged. Rather than risk negotiating the dangerous Dyfi estuary mouth, she turned and headed for Aberystwyth and a seemingly easier harbour entrance. However, she came in too close on the northern approach and was washed on to Ro Fawr. As she wallowed in the surf a few yards from shore, the hatch opened and the heavy cargo of culm spilled out and covered Evan Hughes, who drowned, but two of the crew were rescued. It is the only Borth subject painted by the Aberystwyth Primitive.

The expanding slate industry in the second half of the 19th century was to provide Aberdyfi with the export cargo that helped to create its heyday as a port and, by association, the apogee of Borth's maritime achievements in connection with the port. From the time of Edward I and beyond the Elizabethan age, slate was increasingly used by those who could afford it. In the 1590s over a quarter of a million slates were exported from Anglesey to Ireland. Although slate was part of the export cargoes of Aberdyfi as early as the 18th century, there was not a high demand locally for the product as the population was pastoral and static with no substantial building enterprises being undertaken. It was not until the industrial age really took off that the capital investment needed to exploit slate would bring attractive profits. Prior to this time even the cost of carriage to the coast could be prohibitive. In 1765 Blaenau Ffestiniog's slate was carried by packhorse from its mountainous location along primitive tracks and then put on small boats which took it down waterways to the sea. Later narrow guage railways provided an appropriate solution to such convolutions.

The export of Welsh slate had been primarily from Pembrokeshire and Caernarfonshire, but from the 1840's there was a rapid increase in the number of quarries in south Merionethshire. The years 1840 to 1885 were Aberdyfi's heydays with shipbuilding increasing along with the growing prosperity. Although the slate industry was primarily funded by English investors, shipping affairs were managed by locals, and here Borth people played a substantial role as mariners, investors and shipowners. The local schooner fleet expanded to accomodate the exporting of this cargo. Since everything was moved by hand, a schooner's cargo could be loaded or unloaded in a reasonable time. Slate production had increased dramatically after 1831 with the repeal of a repressive slate duty. Prior to this time, slates leaving West Wales for a destination such as London incurred a duty comparable to the cargo's total value, thus doubling the cost. In 1842 another boost to trade occurred after the German city of Hamburg suffered a disasterous fire. Large amounts of Welsh slates went to re-roof this city and, as a result, the trade extended to other north European ports. For a time there were strong maritime trading links between west Wales and Germany.

The arrival of the railway system in west Wales was perceived initially as being beneficial to ports such as Aberdyfi. The reality was that it became, over four decades, its destroyer by providing a swifter, safer and cheaper freight service. Everywhere, sail was being superceded by steam and the new:

alternative in the shape of the steam engine - ashore and afloat - was already a growing menace before the Slate Boom had begun; and to the shrewd ones it was already clear that, do what she might to refine herself and grease her bottom, the sailing ship was an anachronism (Morgan, 1948, p.187)

The railway's fatal stranglehold saw the port go into decline and finally collapse by the end of the century. Aberdyfi's demise meant that those Borth men who had been working there had to look elsewhere for work. Fortunately, they were already well equipped to do so as they had widespread family connections at other ports. Many Borth mariners had already gained employment on deepwater sailing ships. Amongst them were Captains Edward Edwards, the *Euridyce*, John Lewis, the *Snowdon*, Evan L. Davies, the *Zinnia*, John Lloyd, the *Dora Ann*, David Lloyd, the *Zimmi*, Lewis Williams, the *Coromandel* and David Williams, the *Ivanhoe*. Their seamanship was formidable when one considers that Captain Evan Jenkins was only just thirty when he commanded some of the largest sailing vessels afloat. Also in his thirties, Captain Richard Edwards was in charge of the 2,268 ton, four masted sailing barque *Holt Hill*.

At this time, even though sail was giving way to steam, Borth seafarers took the changes in their stride. Many of the men commanded and crewed steamers owned by the Cambrian Steam Navigation Company Ltd. of Aberystwyth. Although this company's ships were too big to enter Aberystwyth harbour, the crews were recruited locally. Captain William Francis of Borth commanded the *S.S. Glantivy* in 1891. Villagers John Hughes, Richard and John Jones served on the *Glanhafren* in 1893 (Troughton, 1997, pp.39 – 42). In a photograph of the *Glanhafren's* crew of 1894 the sitter in the front row on the far right is Borth man John Richards who was master of the schooner Catherine twenty or so years earlier. The *Harrovian's* master in 1901 was Captain Richard James of Borth. For the next sixty years Borth's seafarers continued in the maritime tradition, including service throughout two world wars. As they had done in sail, they again provided a vital contribution in the age of steam, serving as masters and crew members on a variety of vessels including tramp steamers, oil tankers and luxury liners. Their story is yet to be told.

HERRING FISHING

Sgadan y Borth, sgadan y Borth   (Herrings of Borth, Herrings of Borth
Dau lygad ym mhob corff   Two eyes in each body)

This was the ancient Borth herring-sellers' cry that once reverberated through the autumn air in local villages. The fish sellers and their herring laden carts travelled from Borth via Ynyslas calling at the farms on the way to Llangynfelin. By the time they arrived at Tre'r-ddol Taliesin and Talybont, the price of the fish was increased slightly. Village children carried baskets of herrings on foot along the circuitous route up over Rhiw Fawr to the farms of Ty Du, Brynbala, Brynbwl, Moel Cerni, Ty Llechwedd Bach, Rhydmeirionydd, Rhoscellan, Wileirog Isaf, Maenuwch, Wileirog Uchaf, Ffos Y Gravel Isaf, Ffos Y Gravel Uchaf, Blaunwaen, Cilolwg, Rhiwlas, Tynewydd and Tir Helig. Others took their catch by handcart to Glanwern and from there to the farms of Felinwern, Glanleri, Tynsimnau, Penwern and back to the hamlet of Dolybont. They would call at Felinfawr, then over the Leri up to Henllys Farm and Bryneithyn Farm and on to the cottages at Taicannol. From there to Brynllys Farm and finally Pantydwn Farm. Returning home, those on foot crossed the bog via Ynys Gwaethfoed fording the Leri at Ynys Fergi, whilst those with a cart crossed the river back near Brynllys ... all accessing the village via the Rhyd Road.

It is certain that the herring *(clupea harengus)* created and sustained the settlement of Borth, and many others on the Welsh seaboard. This fish remained an emotive pivotal point in village life until the early twentieth century. The Celtic peoples held this potentially life-saving creature in high esteem. The Welsh for herring is ysgadenyn and in the plural ysgadan. The 'y' is dropped nowadays, so it is like the Irish spelling, scatan or sgadan. For the Manx it was skeddan and in Cornish guidn. The herring had become part of the people's psyche and they perceived that a threat to this natural bounty was also a threat to them. So much so that in 1878, fisherman Humphrey Owen of Aberystwyth blamed the decline of herrings on the fact that previous gluts of this fish had resulted in them being used as manure - an insult to nature (Buckland & Walpole, 1878-9).

The catching of this bounty of the sea was so crucial to Borth villagers' survival that at times it had Biblical connotations as it echoed Christ's life and work amongst the Galilean fishermen. In the fervour of the Methodist Revival, the herring for many became a symbol of the Host; the body of Christ. It conjured up images of this fish as a kind of manna that alleviated the spiritual and physical hunger. No doubt haunting the memories of the people were the spectres of previous famines. These themes inspired the late author A. E. Richards (1905-1982), whose plays and short stories such as *Master Mariner* and *Who'll Buy My Fresh Herrings* are redolent of Borth as he based his characters and themes on village history and folklore. His works include these religious considerations, evolving from Borth folk's dependence on sea harvests when he stated "The shining herring shoal is a miracle in the evening of the year" (Richards, 1950, p.5). Many a version is told in Borth of how the congregation of a local chapel was led by the preacher past Pengoitan Farm and up to the fields bordering the cliff opposite today's Francis Road. The whole gathering knelt on the ground and the preacher the prayers exhorting the Lord to arrange for the arrival of the already overdue herring. The village was herring-dependant to such a degree that after a poor season in 1898, a local newspaper reported that Borth people would have to suffer a dire winter because of a dismal herring harvest (*Cambrian News*, October 1898).

The first towering headland south of Borth is called Craig y Wylfa, which means Cliff of Vigil. Some have suggested a romantic connection with smuggling, but its primary role, as the name suggests, was its use, especially by the women folk, to watch for the returning fishing boats. A heavy price was paid at times in reaping the herring harvest. In the 1840's four men lost their lives whilst herring drifting, one of whom was the grandfather of Captain John Davies of Maesteg House. The last vigil on Craig y Wylfa took place in 1917 when three Borth men were lost whilst salvaging in the bay; two of them were Betty Doyle and Ronnie Davies' antecedents. In the old days, if the bodies were recovered they would be laid in an open coffin in their homes and a vigil called 'gwylnos' was kept with most of the village, including the children, gathering in relays to pay their respects. Upon leaving, money would be left in a collection bowl for the grieving widow or parents. These tough fishermen of Borth have been described thus :

> The men who worked in this way for a bare sustenance, buying bread for their families with their lives often, developed qualities of courage, piety, resourcefulness and thrift hardly to be met with under gentler conditions. Like the marram grass, the plant most familiar to them on their exposed foreshore, they adapted themselves, had to adapt themselves, in order to live (Morgan, 1948, p.196).

Historically, when the herring fishing began in September around Michaelmas, the Borth boats would cast their nets and drift south-west, aided by an ebbing tide, as far as the edge of Sarn Cynfelyn, and often, weather permitting, as far as Caergwyddno (Gwyddno's Fort, or now, The Patches). In the old days, candles or lamps were lit and left in the back windows of the cottages to guide the fishermen home. If there rose a 'môr tir' (ground swell), prior to the boats' return, especially toward evening which falls quickly in the late autumn, bonfires were lit along the Borth shore by the womenfolk and children. In these dangerous conditions, to save foundering in the surf, boats could run into the Dyfi or, prior to the 1820s, the river Leri.

Light easterlies blowing offshore, signalled by a dark cloud bank appearing above the surrounding inland hills are the ideal weather conditions for herring fishing. This cloud formation which can last for days, is called 'dwyren penddu' which means 'black eastern cloudhead'. Also at herring time, farmers on the inland fringes of Cors Fochno would take advantage of these easterly winds and burn off vast areas of the fenland to encourage fresh pasture for the following spring. This was an annual event in my youth and it was an amazing sight to see a line of fire moving slowly towards the village, to eventually halt at the barrier provided by the river Leri. I recall on one of these occasions whilst herring fishing at night, seeing the village from out at sea silhouetted against the red glowing sky... an unforgettable experience.

All along Ceredigion's coastline a great flurry of activity was engendered by the herring season. By the 1700s there were nearly one hundred fishing smacks from Newquay, Aberaeron, Aberystwyth and Borth operating in the area. The visual records of the local herring fisheries are scant except for the work of Alfred Worthington (1837-1927). Born in Kent, he came to live in Aberystwyth on his physician's instructions in 1875. Amongst his many interests, photography and painting of local scenes were to become his main preoccupations. He undertook a series of marine paintings and his oil painting *The Herring Fleet*, is a rare depiction of local fishing practices. The centuries old sight he painted would vanish in the next few decades. Also amongst his prodigious output of local scenes was a panoramic view of the village, *Borth from Rhiw Fawr*.

Today, adjacent to Pengoitan House where Cliff Road begins, is a little seating area and beach access which has always been known as The Slip, referred to in Welsh as Y Slip. This ramp, whose remains can be seen in old photographs, facilitated the launching of the herring boats. The situation began to change with the decline of local boat ownership and a new road built along the front in the 1890s. For those who had no boats there was always the beach where they could set their herring nets. This was a time-honoured practice, especially enjoyed by widows and the cockle and shrimping women. In ancient times with the scarcity of boats, herring were so numerous that they were easy to catch on the beach itself. In times of such abundance, boats often anchored their nets overnight just offshore adjacent to the village, making them easier to retrieve the next morning. This was often practiced by myself and others such as Gethin and Jack Evans, Sid Clare, Alun Evans and Ronnie Davies in the 1960's and 70's, especially after several previous fruitless all night drifts. Fishing just offshore, one had to ensure the nets weren't too deep otherwise they dragged in the sand. This caused problems especially if the net was allowed to concertina during slack water at the tidal change. This encouraged crabs and thornback rays to feed on the trapped herrings, so cut down nets were used. Old nets were often the ones that were set on the beach.

In 1969 I caught five hundred splendid herrings just on the beach under the lifeboat station and gave many to the locals amongst whom was Gareth Raw-Rees of Tynparc. He told me they were the finest herrings he had tasted since his boyhood at Brynbwl farm. Each was coated in a silvery skin that he called 'pais arian' (silver petticoat). According to his wife, Mari, he became quite covetous of these particular fish and not at all keen on sharing them, which was so uncharacteristic of him. Others who instinctively recognised the quality of these particular fish were Glenys Griffiths of Gwastad Farm and David Llewelyn Lewis, who as children remembered and appreciated what this fish had meant to the village. The herring still had a noticeably powerful hold on that particular generation. Hugh Hughes, known as Hugh 'Boston', recalls that in the spring of 1951, on his return from sea, his mother had kept some herrings for him from the previous November. They were nearly disintegrating when she took them out of the 'pair pridd', earthenware pancheon, to fry for him. He remembers their taste with intense emotion (H. Hughes, pers. comm. 2003). The intangible hold of the herring affected Sid Clare to such a degree that even knowing the herring shoals were off Aberystwyth where he kept his boat, he would still journey north to Borth to first cast his nets. He was keeping a kind of covenant with the long past (S. Clare, pers. comm. 2003).

These fish could cause passions to run high Jac Richards still smouldered with indignation 80 years after being deprived of an extra herring in his childhood. His mother, as was the custom amongst the congregation of Soar Chapel, invited a visiting preacher home for supper after an evening's service. It was November and soused herring was the dish served up. The preacher had a large herring and Jac a small one. However, there was one left over which Jac thought would be his as surely, good manners and methodistic frugality, meant the preacher would refuse the extra fish. Alas, it was not to be and to Jac's chagrin his mother served the plump herring to her guest. "Rwy ddim wedi madde i'r diawl hyd heddi"... "I have not forgiven the devil to this day" (J. Richards, pers. comm. 2000)

The totalling of the herring catches was done numerically and not by weight. A meise of herrings locally is 500 fish. However, this varies in different regions of Britain, as some included extra fish as tally devices to denote the scores and the hundreds; similarly there was a long hundred, which often meant a total of 124 fish. Youngsters in Borth were encouraged to become involved in the herring harvest by using a local system called 'sgadan bys' (finger herrings), where a child after helping to land the catch on the beach would be rewarded with as many herrings as they were able to hold in each hand, allowing for one fish per finger. This was a maximum of 10 fish for those who could manage to carry them in the cold and often freezing weather. For small children 2 in each hand was about the limit. Jac Richards often recalled receiving the sgadan bys bounty from my great grandfather David Davies. It is interesting to note that in the records of Morfa School of May 21st of 1881 some boys were absent from school because they were apparently helping in gathering blackberries and herring fishing! Herring fishing in May? No person with local knowledge person would accept that. Herding unicorn would have been more believable!

The herring dependent villagers' precarious existence is nowhere more succinctly described than in *Brief Glory*:

In these tenements, precariously poised between ancient bog and ancient sea, poised on a barrier of sand and pebbles which the pounding surf had raised, it was always either a fast or a feast, oftenest the former. Herring was the main harvest, for of gardens there were few if any, and bog yielded nothing but peat for kindling; and since it was decreed by Nature that even herring should only enter the Bay during the season of storm around Michaelmas it was no easy harvest-home (Morgan, 1948, p.196).

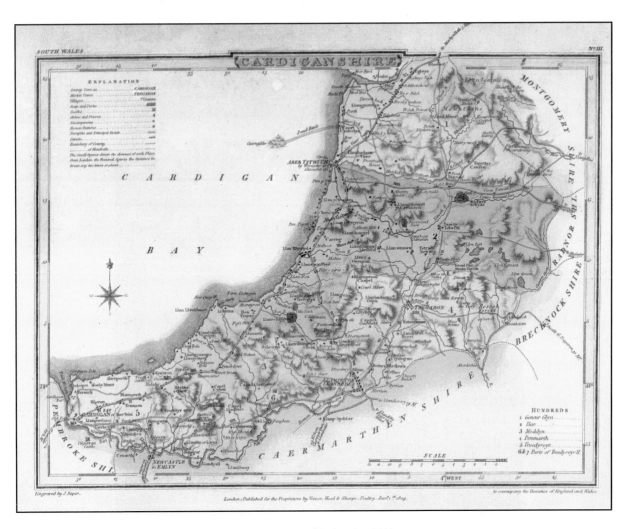

11. Roper, J. *Map of Cardiganshire*, 1809

12. Portrait of captain David Davies

13. Drusus, *barque, Captain David Rees, Borth.*

14. Holt Hill, *barque, Captain Richard Edwards*

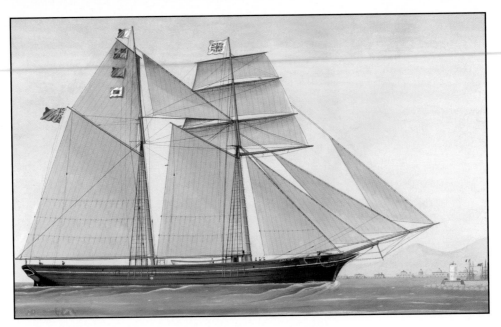

15. Pilgrim, *Schooner, Captain John Davies*

16. Pluvier, *Schooner, Captain Thomas Davies Borth.*

17. Charlotte, Brigantine, Captain Richard Jones

18. S.S. Eira, Captain William Richards

19. The Herring Fleet

20. View of Borth from Rhiw Fawr

21. Wallog Limekiln

22. Dragnetting at Borth

23. Looking south from Morfa Borth

24. Aberwennol looking south

25. Craig y Delyn

26. Ogof y Delyn

27. Carreg Felen

28. Clifftop Quarry, Brynbala

29. Carreg Fach

30. Carreg y Traeth

BORTH BOATS

In the 19th century Richard Lewis constantly prayed for a big herring catch and set forth to achieve this in the aptly named *John Wesley*… he was covering all options! John Jones had a more exotically named craft, the *Sancho Panza*. Others had historic names: Waterloo and the *Black Prince*. Some conjure up a delicate craft like the beautifully named *Lily*, or the Biblically inspired *James*. However, I can only find one fishing boat named after the village, and this was the *Borth Lass*, skippered by John Edwards in the 1870s.

The traditional Borth fishing boats were up to 25 feet long in keel length and the design had been developed locally from the mid 1750s. This boat type has now been credited with being unique amongst Welsh boats of their kind in having three masts. There was a small soch (cuddy or forecastle), where in the fishermen could take turns sheltering during the often freezing conditions. When fishing commenced they threw the stone ballast gathered from the beach overboard and then removed the central mast. This created space amidships that allowed mobility and room for the wet and hopefully fish-laden nets to be piled for the home journey. There is also a more practical reason that written sources do not mention, and that is that these transom sterned boats had to be rowed from the central point backwards keeping their bow pointing out into the surf on their return to the shore to prevent capsizing. On some boats possibly all three masts may have been removable, which at times and under certain conditions could be even more convenient, especially when negotiating heavy surf during reverse rowing landing procedures. This boat design was supposedly taken to Aberystwyth around 1840, which coincided with the closure of the sea mouth entrance of the river Leri. This unique Borth type boat is only visually recorded in photographs taken at Aberystwyth.

From about 1880 less complicated rigs were increasingly used, as can be seen in a photograph of a boat on Borth beach seventy years later in 1910. An earlier photograph taken in 1890 shows a number of traditional fishing boats drawn up on the shingle bank near Evelwen House, one with a fore and aft rig is drying its sails. This photograph was taken from a field just behind the old County Primary School, today's Community Centre. Around the same time an 1894 oil painting by James Burrell Smith (1824-1897), in the private collection of Peter and Celia Holt, titled *At Borth near Aberystwyth*, depicts a local coastal scene, and allowing for artistic licence, is undoubtedly Aberwennol. It includes in the foreground a woman with baskets alongside a local fishing boat up on the shingle; it has one mast, so presumably it also had a fore and aft rig. There were small open row boats with a single sail, which operated offshore within three or four miles of the village, such as the one in the photograph of Jac 'Shami' Davies the elder, catching a mackerel off Carreg Felen around 1910.

Up to 1900 Borth's primary role in the context of herring fishing had been to provide the village and the surrounding hamlets and farms with this seasonal harvest. From that time there was a rapid decline in herring fishing, and with it boat ownership in Borth. In the following list of 19th century Borth fishing boats, the fourth entry *James*, had three sprit sails and was the last of the unique Borth fishing boat type with a removable centremast.

Boats	Owners	Dates of Registration
Bee	William Edwards	1872

John Wesley	Richard Lewis	1874
Sancho Panza	John Jones	1875
James	John Davies	1875
Borth Lass	John Edwards	1877
Ann Ellen	John Davies	1877
John Wesley	Hugh Jones	1879
Hope	Richard Jenkins	1879
The Black Prince	James Williams	1879
Ann Jane	David Hughes	1881
Maria	Hugh Jones	1889
Clara	Thomas Williams	1892
Lily	John Davies	1894
Elfrida	John Hughes	1896
Elsie	Evan Davies	1896
Lizzie	George Dutton	1899
The Fisher	George Dutton	1899
Hope	John William Dutton	1899
Mary Ann	John Richards	1900
Bird	William Williams	1900
Hope	John David Jones	1900
Seagull	John William Walton	1900
Lorne	John Hughes	1900

Evan Davies listed above, known as Evan 'Mona' was a superb seaman. He was witnessed sailing the 22 foot *Elsie* in and out of the sea defence groynes effortlessly pulling up the centreboard in the shallowing water, whilst at the same time hauling in his two mackerel lines. He then tacked away from the shore recasting his lines, dropping his centreboard, he sailed out. This manoevere he continued in and out of the then sea defences all the way from Upper Borth to Ynyslas (J. Richards, pers. comm. 1970). No doubt, he like other village boys, some as young as five, had begun his seagoing experience in local herring boats. Many had graduated to coastal trading sloops by the age of eight, which honed skills to a remarkable degree. No wonder Borth produced a prodigious number of able mariners.

By 1930 there were only a few small rowing boats left in the village which, as well as being used for fishing, acted as lifeboats. Ronnie Davies' antecedents at Morfa Borth, possessed one of the few boats left in the village in the 1930s and this was often used as a rescue boat. This was in response to the growing number of bathing misshaps with the increase of summer visitors to the village. In 1946, near Trwyn Cyntaf, on a stormy July day, with a gale blowing from the southwest, the ebbing tide created a viscious undertow which swept a bather out to sea. John Arnold Davies, owning the only boat at the southern end of the village, went to the rescue. Having launched the boat in the shallows, he was imploring someone to jump aboard as it was all he could do, even with his experience, to manage the boat in the treacherous conditions. Of the people that had gathered on the beach, only Pamela Richards had the courage to join him. This young woman had only recently arrived in the village as the bride of the author A. E. Richards. Just before boarding the boat she turned to the male bystanders and snapped; "call yourselves men"? The rescue was successfully completed by this duo followed by a hazardous return ashore, complicated by the need to row astern through the pounding surf (M. Davies, pers. comm. 1960). Later, largely thanks to Aran Morris, a lifeboat was stationed at Borth which was far better equipped to deal with these situations than the heavy transom sterned boat featured in the 1946 rescue.

Having to adapt to the difficult conditions encountered when working from a storm beach meant that Borth men became an inventive lot. John Arnold Davies, who began his working life at 14 as a blacksmith at Penybont before going to sea with his uncle Captain John Davies, of Gloucester House, used his metalworking skills to good effect in a maritime context. He made a metal false keel that was slung over the side after the boat had been rowed past the surf. It came up under the boat's keel and was tied at bow and stern. With this in place the boat could carry a good spread of canvas enabling her to be speedier and more manoeverable. He and his father also designed a boat transporting device made out of light cartwheels that had a bridged axle with a long pole joined to its centre. From this axle there hung a strong canvas covered chain sling. This was pushed into the shallows and with the pole in an upright position the sling lay on the sand releasing the boat. Conversely when the pole was pulled down the sling moved up and lifted the boat which could now be moved along the beach. The ability to grasp and turn the big spoked wheel was a great advantage. This device was superior to the later car wheeled vehicles that came into fashion in the 1940s, which when bogged down in the sand were difficult to move manually.

From the 1940s and for the next two decades, there was scarcely a boat in the village. Then for a number of years in the 1960s, Gethin and Jack Evans ran the 28 foot fishing vessel *Shandala* from Aberystwyth Harbour, and sometimes from Leri mouth at Ynyslas. From then on there was quite a flurry of local boat owners, some fishing commercially and others for pleasure. Jac Richards and Gareth Raw-Rees, owned the 36 foot ex-lifeboat *Merch Y Môr*. Also at this time, Ronnie Davies and Sid Clare fished from a 16 foot bass boat and the larger 26 foot *Ynys Enlli* moored at Aberystwyth and often used for herring fishing. Alan Wells and Christopher Mee had a converted cutter that was based in the Leri. The Davies brothers, Derek, Teddy and Glyn, fished from a 15 foot open boat. Alun Evans and I owned an 18 foot dory, *Glas Y Dorlan*, which was ideal for Borth beach conditions. Kai and Anna Hubbard, and later Louis Delahaye, fished from small boats. All this was mixed fishing, including lobster, crab, mackerel, bass and herring. From the mid 1970s, David Samson has fished professionally from a large open boat based at Borth, assisted nowadays by Peter Williamson. As well as crustaceans, bass, turbot and mackerel, this duo harvest cockles and mussels from the Dyfi estuary. Recently others have begun to fish professionally, including the partners John Matthews and Michael Smith, using a small open boat, and Paul Burke"Abbo", working from a coble. Lobster in now the main catch of these village fishermen and not herring

31. Borth designed fishing boat, circa 1890

32. Borth designed boat at Aberystwyth

33. Fishing boat at Borth, circa 1910

34. Boat with cartwheel carriage, circa 1940

LOCAL FISHING PRACTICES

Borth women of yesteryear were a hardy lot, especially those who gathered cockles and fished for shrimps. The shrimpers pushed their nets up and down Borth beach from Trwyn Cyntaf all the way to Ynyslas and around into the estuary. Sometimes the cockle women would carry a trident to stab for flounders or any other flatfish in the estuarine shallows. There is a story about a particularly tough, feisty, pipe-smoking lady who lived in a cottage opposite today's Westward Ho who after a hard days cockling was in the habit of taking a drink at the Friendship Inn. On one occasion, having run out of money but still thirsty, she walked back home to get some more from her husband. He refused to give her the money in his pocket, so she changed tack and started canoodling with him. Feigning passion, she reached into his trouser pocket, to what he presumed was to be a furtherance of pleasurable activity; but instead she tightened and twisted her grasp leaving him flat on his back defenceless. Going through his pockets the cockle lady took the money and returned to continue her revelry at the Inn.

Around 1860, cockle lady Ann Hughes regularly trudged over the vast Dyfi estuary sands. This lady reputedly carried a sixty pound sack filled with cockles on her back from Traeth Maelgwn to her tiny cottage which was somewhere opposite the house known today as Evelwen. Occasionally, weather permitting, she and other cockle ladies would cook the shellfish on a driftwood fire at Ynyslas. Doing this and removing the shells lightened the load. Ann took the cooked cockles eight miles to Aberystwyth to be sold for a penny a cup. With the money, she would sometimes buy three or four loaves of bread and on her return to Borth keep one for herself and sell the others. On a typical day she, like the other cockling ladies, would have walked a total of approximately twenty miles. Somewhere near Ann Hughes's cottage, under the stones there may be a midden heap formed from the many cockle excursions she undertook. Her cottage could have been the earthwalled one seen in the background of the photograph titled *Native Captains Borth*. An unpublished 1949 short story by A. E. Richards, *Home For Good*, is about such a cockle woman and her hard life, that includes a death at sea involving a wrecked Borth schooner. The following risque ditty concerning the cockle ladies was told to me by Mr and Mrs Davies of Dolclettwr Hall Farm:

> *Cocos a wyau*   *Cockles and eggs*
> *A bara ceirch tenau*   *with thin oat bread*
> *Sy'n gwneud i hen ladis*   *makes old ladies*
> *Godi eu cynffonnau*   *lift up their tails*

Borth native Anna Hubbard, in her role as lifeboat crew member in the 1980's, dragnetter and a keen fisherwoman, has in a sense continued Borth women's traditional connections with the sea. Her daughter Sian was also a lifeboat crew member in the early 1990's.

Rockpool fishing for lobster, crab and prawns is a long established practice at Borth. The small beach just before Trwyn Pellaf was the furthest point at which Canon Llewelyn Jenkins went fishing. He was a keen crabber and would often catch a substantial amount of these crustaceans on his fishing beat, mainly around Trwyn Canol (Middle Point). In the 1950's

Canon Jenkins retired to his native Borth and lived in Rock House. He was from a typical Borth farming and maritime background, whose family homes were Pengoitan Farm and Rock House. His father, master mariner John Jenkins, born 1843, and his mother Phebe, born 1844, had five sons and one daughter who were all brought up at Rock House. The daughter Rebecca, married Captain David Davies of Borth. The eldest son Richard became a shipbroker in Liverpool and his brother David a ship's engineer. The other three brothers, Thomas, John and Llewelyn had successful careers in the church. Canon Jenkins always wore his ecclesiastical apparel, which included a wide-brimmed hat that I and my boyhood friends were convinced was a cowboy hat. He looked as if he had just stepped out of Anthony Trollope's 'Barchester Towers' as Septimus Harding. He obviously suffered from bad eyesight, as one lens of his spectacles was completely blacked-out and the other was so thick it enlarged his eyeball.

When I first met Canon Jenkins on fishing forays in the 1950's, I was a little frightened of the black-dressed man with his cyclopean eye, who prawned with an improbably clumsy-looking net, which was a museum piece even then. It was typical of a type made in Borth in the 1800's described as "an enormous implement, about ten foot long, consisting mainly of a young ash tree and weighing umpteen pounds" (Beadnell, 1920). It was known in Welsh as a ciprhwyd, rhwyd meaning net, whilst cip comes from cipio which means to steal or snatch. This was also the term also used to denote a larger, more egg-shaped net which was designed especially for lobster catching. Canon Jenkins's net was made from a seven-foot-long forked bough which was stripped of its bark and long bleached with age. A ring of iron was attached to the forked end and the bag net was slung from this. The pole wood had not been dressed or smoothed, so it retained the contortions of natural growth and was thicker toward the base. The net pole's twists and bends may have been selected so as to fit the user, just like a scythe handle. These archaic nets always looked heavy and awkward to me. It may even be unique to Borth, since the Aberystwyth Primitive's painting *Aberystwyth Rocks* circa 1850, shows a different design of circular hoop net with thin straight handles being used for rockpool fishing. A 1910 photograph shows a young A. E. Richards, with a rock fisherman from the Jenkins family of Pengoitan Farm, Borth, holding such a net. They are photographed outside the entrance to Twll Ladi Wen.

When I was about twelve, Canon Jenkins and I were comparing our respective catches at Trwyn Canol when he said that at my age he'd gone fishing with his uncle on a particular day, in the previous century, when there had been a phenomenal spring tide. Amazingly they were able to walk from Trwyn Cyntaf around to Aberwennol Bay along the exposed sand outside the rockshelf. They had literally picked up a dozen or so lobsters, which seemed equally surprised by the freakish low tide. The Canon wistfully remembered seeing their long red feelers peeking out from under boulders and out of crevices (Jenkins, pers. comm. 1956). Needless to say, this story fired my imagination. For years afterwards, I dreamt in vain of such a tide, where lobsters were plentiful and easily accessible.

From early spring through to autumn many different types of prawn arrive in waves to the coastal rockpools of Borth. Trwyn Pellaf in particular has always attracted them, and being within sight of the village was the furthest point that a youngster was first allowed to fish alone. I recall innumerable occasions when I would watch Jac Richards fish one of his favourite spots, which is the boulder on the sand by this headland. He had an uncanny knack of knowing when the first prawns of the season were present. He maintained that one should fish after the first two calm days in March so as to catch the newly arrived red/brown type of prawn that he referred to as the "big mahogany ones". The favourite prawning location of the 'Shami' Davies family, Jack and sons Glyn and Ronnie, was around the two large weed-wigged boulders on the northern side of Aberwennol bay. Others I remember were Dic Hughes, a trywn Pellaf only prawner, Clifford Jones, who went no further than Carreg Mulfran and Aran Morris who always went as far as Carreg Fach, near Wallog, in search of his main quarry, the lobster .

My late uncle, David Davies, recalled that among the rock fishermen were many retired sea captains. As a boy he remembered them as being silent and almost sullen in this pursuit, affected no doubt by a strict allocation of fishing areas - to encroach on another's territory was a serious breach of etiquette. The men's wives would often be encouraged to exaggerate their spouse's catch just to raise the ire of the other fishermen (D. Davies, pers. comm. 2001). Now, the number of knowledgeable native pursuers of prawn and lobster by hand-net and hook has dwindled to just a few. To the north of Craig y Delyn, set high in the cliff face is a row of white stones called Cerrig Gwynion. Few realise that they have been used for centuries as markers to locate fruitful lobster holes on the rock shelves below. At Trywn Pellaf there are pools named after the men who favoured them such as Pwll Tom Hughes and Pwll Dai Dafis. The latter was named after my great grandfather, who was fishing it around 1870. The former pool was named after Thomas Hughes who lived with his widowed mother at what was in my youth Castle Stores.

Georgie Dutton, a local character who had once owned the fishing boats *Lizzie* and *The Fisher*, was a keen prawner. Even in old age he would leap into the deep pool at the outer edge of Trwyn Canol, to pre-soak himself, declaring "Oh sweet Sir Garnet" as the cold water enveloped him. Apparently Sir Garnet was a character in a popular novel at the beginning of the 20th century (J. Richards, pers. comm. 1970). George Dutton had a penchant for jumping into things. He was once engaged to help David Hughes clean out the cesspit at Boston House. All the seaside dwellings at Morfa Borth had a cesspit in their pallisaded backyards. This was a dry stone walled inverted cone that allowed continual seepage down through the shingle bank. The job began with the pebbles being cleared away to reveal the wooden baulk cover which was removed to access the pit. The cesspool was duly cleaned out at high tide for obvious reasons. With this stage completed Dutton asked for some of his fee in advance and promising to return later in the evening to finish the job. David Hughes woke up early the next morning and decided to close off the cesspit himself rather than wait for his helper to turn up. Lo and behold there was Georgie Dutton fast asleep at the bottom of the pit. He'd been to the Friendship Inn after leaving Boston House and returned late at night to finish the job. Obviously fatigued with ale he decided to throw himself in the pit to sleep (H. Hughes, pers. comm. 2003). One wonders if he mumbled "Oh sweet Sir Garnet"on the way down to his stoney bed.

As well as using a net and hook to catch the wily lobster, in ancient times a lobster trap was constructed from a suitable piece of blackthorn cut from a hedgerow. A piece of the main branch at the thick end was cleaned so that a rope could be attached to it. The end of the bush was tied together to form a squat broom-like shape. A hole was driven from the thick end into the middle of the bush. A stone for weight was inserted, and having passed the springy thorns was unable to slip out. Bait was likewise driven into the same tunnel. The entrance passageway was carefully lined with scrap wool gathered from hedgerows. The end result was a wool-lined passageway leading deep into the centre of the blackthorn trap. This was lowered into a pool or gully at low water so it could be fished tidally or if one had access to a boat, dropped off at a suitable location. The lobster was not caught on the thorns, but on the wool strands that became entangled around the many protrusions on its carapace and the joints of its claws and legs.

There is perhaps only one form of fishing that requires no specialist knowledge, equipment or great skill, and that is sprat catching in the autumn. Great shoals of sprats gather in the shallows at Borth beach which can be seen from Rhiw

Fawr as an undulating mass from Trwyn Cyntaf to Ynylsas. They are so numerous that they can sometimes be caught with a bucket at the sea edge. Another way to catch them is at night with a ground swell running. Ideal conditions are around high tide, directly on the sea side of Morfa Borth. All one needs is a torch if there is no moonlight. The procedure is that after each wave any sprats that are cast up on the shingle can be quickly picked up before the next one arrives. I recall the great fun I had in the company of the Davies boys of Elidir, when an evenings sprat catching would inevitably end with some of us with shoes full of water. On some nights one could catch a bucketful. The sprats were dredged in flour and fried, or baked in a pan and provided a delicious meal.

Dragnetting is another local fishing method that has a long history. The practice was handed down to the younger generation when they started as the inside net puller. Jac Richards first began netting with Twm Hughes of Castle Stores, when he was about ten. Twm used to call at Jac's mother's house, much to her disapproval, and tap on the kitchen window calling to him in Welsh, "Come on, I can hear the fish singing. They want us to catch them." The enticement of the term 'singing fish' denotes the use of a device to pre-empt the hardships involved in this fishing method. Twm was always debonair and even when netting wore, of all things, a three piece suit. This much used suit was so stiff with salt that he had to bang it with a stick prior to putting it on. Over all this he wore an overcoat and a sou'wester on his head (M. Brown, pers. comm. 2003).

Thomas Rowley Morris of Gleanor House recalled that in 1898 he and David Davies of Balmoral Cottage, were dragnetting and decided, even though the tide was almost touching Trwyn Canol to go further and have one last big sweep of the beach area just before Trwyn Pellaf. Half way along they realised that they were now being rapidly cut off by the sea, so they dragged the net up over the rocks as they knew there was quite a shoal of fish already trapped. As Mr Morris related, many escaped as the net was being torn on the rocks but the eventual catch was 83 fine sewin. By the time the net was wrapped up the sea was well in and they had to hasten under the cliffs so as to get back to the Slip (T.R. Morris, pers comm, 1963). Mr Morris's son Aran, recalls with affection the old mariner John Robert Jones who lived at Inman Cottage. It was from him that Aran and friends always borrowed a dragnet, inevitably with the same parting proviso, "Byddwch yn ofalus, myndiwch yr hen boncyffion sydd ar yr trath"..." be careful, and mind the old tree stumps on the beach" (A. Morris, pers. comm, 2003). He was of course alluding to the remains of the sunken forest.

Many who had left the village to pursue careers elsewhere would often, on summer visits to their family, immediately set out on one of these fishing forays. No doubt many of those returning natives were re-acquainting themselves with childhood in a beloved place, despite travels or settlement elsewhere. I always knew Glyn Davies was home in summer when I could see two figures dragnetting in the half light of dawn. He and his father Jack 'Shami' Davies would net from the north end all the way to Trwyn Cyntaf and finish at Pwll y Môr, just as it was beginning to fill with the incoming tide. Glyn's brother Ronnie still has the dragnet poles that his family have used for over a hundred years. This family's forebears lived at today's Westward Ho, and can be seen in a photograph where they are grouped on the beach around their boat, the Neena. As a youngster living at White Lion Place, Ronnie would sleep downstairs so as not to miss out on going dragnetting. He was 'bag boy', and often struggled to carry home the fish-filled hessian sack. The catch was varied; skate, thornback ray, blonde ray, turbot, plaice, sole, bass, mullet and sewin. The rays would be cut up on the beach to lighten the load. The skate 'wings' were usually nailed to a shed door or fence so as to facilitate their skinning a day or so later. A bag boy was always cursed by the net pullers if he waded out in the shallows to assess the catch before they did. Plaice up to five pounds and turbot up to twelve pounds in weight were regularly caught up to the 1970s. Ronnie recalls his father telling him that as a boy he would go with family members to the sand dunes if fishing was poor, to set up the net into which the plentiful rabbits there would be driven. This alternative to fishing would be aided with the presence of a whippet named Rosa (R. Davies, pers. comm, 2003).

I, like many others, began my dragnetting 'career' under the tutelage of Bill Edwards. I fished mainly with his sons, Thomas James, David, Michael and Gwilym; the latter as bag boy. The standard 'uniform' for this form of fishing in those days was layers of old coats to keep out the cold. For the outside puller, in deeper water, a flat cap worn backwards was essential to avoid a wavetop sending a flush of cold water down one's neck and back. Fishing was done mainly in the dark and I remember on my first forays imagining that the occasional slippery clay patches that I suddenly trod on were huge stingrays, which resulted in my instinctively jumping up on the pole. Bill Edwards conducted fishing 'business' from the Railway Inn where he would mesmerise visitors with tales of his 'trawlers' full of large catches. The usual fishing method was to begin dragnetting southwards from opposite the Golf Club. Inevitably, when we had reached the back of the village after several pulls there came the sound of Bill Edwards scrambling down the shingle bank onto the beach. As usual, he was exhorting us to go out further. The air would be blue with one of the Edwards boys up to his neck in water telling his father to "bugger off back to the pub" and that he was "out as far as he could go without drowning". Gwilym, as bagboy, was instructed by his father to go round the back of the pub with anything that was caught. Fish other than flatfish or skate were presented in a basket with cabbage leaves and parsley where often mullet would be masquerading as sewin with Bill spinning some improbable yarn to the gullible about them being a strain of local sea trout.

Unwittingly Bill was an environmentally friendly fisherman as there were usually enough holes in the net for a pod of dolphins to pass through and the net poles were like pit props making them difficult to grasp. After four of five hours of hard slog, with only a reasonable amount of fish and having redistributed a ton of seaweed along the beach we'd be given a lecture on our return to headquarters at the Edwards cottage about not going out far enough. Once, in high dudgeon, Thomas James the eldest son replied "I was so far out I started developing an Irish accent". Our clothes were dumped along the old stone wall to be used again, without washing of course. We then stood naked and shivering in the early hours of the morning throwing buckets of warm soapy water over each other. Thankfully, Mrs. Edwards would make a massive pot of tea to warm us up. On the way home smelling like a Grimsby trawler one questioned the sanity of it all. Nevertheless, like many others, I eventually got my own net and enjoyed many a fruitful night's fishing dragging the gravelly bank opposite Wesley Chapel with Jack Evans or Michael Pugh. A later development was the use of a boat. Alun Evans and I would shoot the net from the stern of our boat *Glas y Dorlan*, an 18ft dory, that was ideal in the surf and an improvement on the wet and miserable conditions previously endured.

Dragnetting is still popular and this ancient fishing method can be seen in the right hand foreground of the illustration *Barred Havon* which is a view of Aberystwyth and its fleet of sloops. Dragnetting has also been commemorated in a Medieval Welsh poem:

> *For the seas have I been accustomed*
> *I will walk by sea and river*
> *along the strand with my circled net.*
> (Maredudd ap Rhys, 1430-60)

35. Davies family, circa 1912

36. Jac Shami Davies the elder, circa 1912

37. Jac Shami Davies, the younger, circa 1950

38. The Barred Haven

39. Borth Dragnetters, circa 1930

40. Rocks at Aberystwyth

41. Tom Hughes and his mother, circa 1910

42. "Ted" Richards and Mr. Jenkins at Twll Ladi Wen, 1911

43. Will Sion Dafydd, 1840

44. David Davies of Balmoral, 1928

45. Jack Richards, circa 1978

BORTH STORIES

The sea harvest was a major source of protein supplement for the surrounding hinterland that saw many farms buying masses of herrings to preserve by salting or smoking. Brynllys Farm was famed in the past for its sgadan coch (red herrings). Also over the centuries thousands of Borth herrings must have been smoked at Dolclettwr Hall Farm at Trerddol. One can still see the oak poles set on the right side of the interior of the huge chimney. Here the gutted salted fish would be hung whole to smoke, in Welsh 'i gochi'... to redden. Tradition has it that the massive wooden fireplace lintel at this farm was from a Spanish Armada wrecked locally (Davies, pers. comm. 2003).

Many of Borth's fisherfolk supplemented their livelihood working the fields in exchange for their own row of vegetables. There is reference to this in a story that A.E. Richards told me about his grandmother who, newly wed in 1865, lost her wedding ring while preparing her potato row in Brynllys field. A period of anguish followed where she had to go to great lengths to hide the fact that her wedding ring was missing. Later in the year whilst harvesting her crop she miraculously found the ring. The spirit of this exchange between villagers and farmers continued into modern times, whereby if one helped out on a farm at harvest time, one could traverse the fields for game during the winter. Another, quirky connection between land and sea occured when the French smack *Sans Pareil*, on approaching Aberdyfi, lost a cargo of Magnum Bonum potatoes off Borth beach. From that day, these potatoes became a favourite in the locality, as they were used as seed potatoes for successive harvests.

Many of the farmers, being tenants of local estates, were enterprising enough to invest in shipping. Their contribution was important to maritime endeavours and in turn provided the only investment opportunity they had in their limited world. Despite most of the mariners being related to farming families in the surrounding areas there developed a social divide that saw the seafarers adopting more scornful attitudes toward their rural relatives. It was mostly a game of one-upmanship by the mariners who, having travelled the oceans, saw themselves as being worldly-wise, and few were enamoured of things rural. The following description of Llangrannog is applicable to the larger Borth community.

> *Although most of its early inhabitants moved to the village (Llangrannog) from the surrounding countryside, a dichotomy between an inward-looking agricultural community and an out-ward looking seafaring community soon developed. The difference between a seafaring community and a rural community, although living in close proximity to one another, became so accentuated that it was difficult to believe that they both belonged to the same cultural group* (Jenkins, 1982, p.4).

An early example of this disdainful attitude toward non-maritime folk is the tale of Will Siswrn, (Will Scissors), so named for his cutting remarks in public. He was of farming stock with relatives at Brynbala and Caergywydd farms. His real name was William Richards and he was a master mariner and grandfather of Jac Richards, who told me the following story from the 1890's:

Captain Richards was in chapel on a warm Sunday, totally relaxed, with his eyes closed. A popular young firebrand of a preacher was pontificating about being close to God. Seeing an apparently sleeping member of the congregation, he decided to bridle the recalcitrant by denouncing those who, even in the house of the Lord, were not paying attention or knowing the nearness of Him. As the congregation followed the preacher's stern gaze, Will suddenly opened his eyes. He looked around and instantly understood the situation and, staring straight back into the preacher's eyes, he said, "Pah! I have been nearer the Lord than you will ever be in your pulpit. I have seen his great works and how he manifests himself in the wilds of the vast Atlantic. He has always been with me, guiding me through storms you couldn't imagine in your worst nightmares. Whilst I have felt his great comforting presence, you and your ilk hereabouts have merely sheltered under a hedge.

It was from this incident that the captain earned his nickname. Naturally, the preacher was more circumspect about his own observations in public.

Captain Thomas Davies, master mariner and owner of the schooners *Pluvier* and *Nathaniel*, was on one occasion in his old age, according to Jac Richards, fighting to walk upright against a gale blowing so hard that it threatened to bowl him over. The old captain was implored to be careful in the tempestuous conditions – it was at least force 10. "Tempest? Tempest? This is merely a harbour clearing zephyr," was his retort, which left the youthful listener astounded. He was, according to various local sources, an amorist of note and adored by the ladies. Adding to the legend of his carnal splendour was his reputation for upsetting the moral rectitude of some of the congregation of his chapel by always volunteering to read the lesson, which was inevitably excerpts from *The Song of Solomon*. Young boys nudged and winked, girls giggled, whilst moralists fumed. The testosterone driven captain probably added more to tooth loss by the gnashing he caused, than poor oral hygiene ever did. When he felt that the disapproval of his lasciviousness was mounting, primarily among the farming community, he would atone by swiftly announcing a hymn. Inevitably, it produced another barb aimed at the landlubber by extolling God, in the role of the Great Captain, to look after the mariner (J. Richards, pers. comm. 1970). The hymn's first lines, which I have translated, would be read out with relish:

> On tempestuous seas I sail,
> To a world that is better
> I smile at all the storms
> As my Father is at the helm.
> (Evan Evans, Ieuan Glan Geirionydd).

In his old age, Captain Davies was always chasing passing youngsters away from the front of his house. The reason for this was that he had a beautiful brass strip on the gate step which he lovingly polished every day. He obviously feared that local children would ruin his handiwork; this old seafarer had always wanted everything shipshape. His seamanship was legendary and it was said that dockside workers in many a port would take cover when he was due in. On arrival, he would often decline any assistance such as a tug if conditions were favourable. The crew had to be dressed in their 'Sunday best' and he made his entrance with one hand on the wheel and the other on the massive Bible he carried with him everywhere.

Under reduced sail he would turn and with one deft move he'd bring his vessel gently alongside the quay. He was not as such a God fearing man but rather a God loving man. He certainly had *je ne sais quoi*. He adored ships and women, and they responded unerringly to his firm, loving and knowing hand. Well into his eighties he used to sail his little dinghy up and down Borth Bay, to the increasing concern of his neighbours and family. Finally, pressure from the righteous-minded saw an end to this supposedly unsuitable behaviour by a very senior citizen. One night some persons hacked a hole in his dinghy. Heartbroken, the captain took to his bed and died soon afterwards and many a Borth lady wept.

Although I am too young to remember Captain Davies, I remember his daughter well. I was in the first years of primary school and she was one of the cooks there. In her sixties, she was a deeply tanned lady with the most startling, kindly, blue eyes. I knew from my family that as a child in the 1890's she had stood on the beach opposite her ship-named house, *Nathaniel*, whilst a rowing boat came ashore from her father's schooner to pick her up. Once aboard they sailed south to French and Spanish ports and across the Atlantic to Newfoundland and from there back to the Mediterranean, and then home. Apparently, this diminutive and unassuming lady had often voyaged with her father. There were other intrepid Borth women who went to sea before 1800. The women of the Davies family sailed regularly on vessels such as the *Sarah*, *France* and the *Amity*, skippered by John Davies the Elder and his brother Hugh Davies. In 1822, the wife of Captain Evans gave birth to a son at sea who was appropriately called John Seaborn Evans. Captain Hugh James took his wife Maggie on several voyages, and one of his sons was born at Scranton, U.S.A. in 1872, and another somewhere at sea in 1880. Captain David Jones, born 1838, took his wife Margaret with him on several vessels including the schooner Ceres.

Gwen Lloyd, the other cook at the school was the daughter of a maritime hero. Edward Lewis Lloyd was second officer on the *S.S. Volturno* in 1913 when she left Rotterdam carrying emigrants to Nova Scotia. A violent storm was encountered in the Atlantic and a fire broke out. Part of the vessel was severly damaged affecting wireless communication. The fire had already claimed a fifth of the passengers when Edward Lloyd climbed up the damaged foremast and made repairs so that an S.O.S. could be sent out. During this process he severly burnt his hands, arms and legs, but his actions prevented a potential catastrophe (D.Lloyd, pers. comm. 2003).

The sea took its toll on ships and lives often within sight of home. In 1853 the Borth smack *Eleanor & Betsey* foundered after attempting to enter the Dyfi estuary in difficult conditions. Luckily Captain Hugh Morgan and his crew got off safely by boat. The dangerous entrance into the Dyfi continued to prove treacherous, and in 1857 the ill-fated Venus, a Borth owned and crewed sloop carrying a cargo of limestone from Caernarvon, over-ran its approach to the Dyfi pushed by a westerly gale. Unfortunately the elderly sloop got into difficulties, and in an attempt to beach the vessel it struck the bar south of the Dyfi river entrance and foundered. Captain Thomas Davies was the only survivor on this tragic November day. Later on the same day another Borth sloop the *Britannia* managed to get safely into Aberdyfi despite the difficult conditions. On the 28th of February 1867 a Borth owned and run schooner the *Gratitude* captained by Richard Jones was wrecked on the Dyfi bar, fortunately without loss of life.

The *Venus* skipper Thomas Davies is seen in several photographs and in his old age he became a sort of village crier. Folklore has it that he clung on to his Newfoundland dog who brought him safely to shore beneath Moelynys. Leaving the captain, the dog ran along the beach to sound the alarm. The canine inclusion may have been a fashionable embellishment, as in the 19th century stories concerning dog bravery centred on the Newfoundland breed, popularised by the paintings of Sir Edwin Lanseer (Lewery, 1991, p.31). Two men as well as the ten year old nephew of the Captain drowned. The young boy's body was not found for ten days and was so facially disfigured that he could only be recognised by a burn mark on the back of his hand. Such tragic loss deeply affected the women folk of the village and especially the boy's mother who in this case was not allowed to see her son's body. Another tragic story centres around a father and son. In 1880 the schooner *Meirion Lass* was bought by John Morgan of Borth for his only son David. Before the year was out, on the 28th December, young Captain David Morgan was lost overboard. His grief stricken father sold the vessel soon after. There was also heartbreak for Captain James of Borth, born 1845, when he lost his fifteen year old son who fell overboard from the *Dovey Belle* whilst the schooner was lying off Gravesend in 1897. This death heralded the end of the James family association with this vessel. The drowned boy's grandfather Captain John James, born 1813, commanded the *Dovey Belle* in the 1860's. Strangely some records (Morgan 1947, p.182) associate this ship with Captain John Williams as master and owner. One wonders if in fact there could have been two *Dovey Belles* as historian Lewis Lloyd speculated.

There were other quirky accidents involving Borth vessels. Captain John Simon from Borth, the son of the previously mentioned John Simon, surrendered his certificate in 1917 because he was apparently too old and infirm to continue seafaring. This Captain John Simon was born in 1843 and served on the *Cuerero* from 1883-7 and the *Ellen Catherine* in 1888. He was master of the 73 ton schooner *Lizzie Jane* when it was rammed by the *Ann Jane*, a schooner captained by James Morgan of Borth. The *Lizzie Jane* had been sheltering in the lee of the Pembrokeshire coast waiting for a favourable wind. The *Ann Jane* had the same idea and unfortunately rammed the other schooner. John Simon and the crew of three jumped onto the *Ann Jane* thinking their vessel was sure to sink. Next day there was no sign of the *Lizzie Jane*; she had drifted across the Irish Sea during the night and beached on the Arklow sands. All this was recorded in a court case in which John Hughes of Glasfryn House, Borth, owner of the *Lizzie Jane*, won £489/4/0 damages from Robert Lewis of Barmouth, the owner of the *Ann Jane* (Cambrian News, March 6th, 1886). In D.W. Morgan's account of the misshap it was the *Lizzie Jane* that rammed the *Ann Jane* (D.W. Morgan, pp.238-9, 1948). Perhaps Morgan's version was coloured by the fact that his father, James Morgan, was the skipper of the *Ann Jane*. Captain John Simon was involved in another incident when his schooner *Ellen Roberts* ran aground; fortunately again, there was no loss of life. Simon is not a common surname, although there was an Evan Simon in Llandre in the mid 19th century and also a Daniel Simon at Newquay who built the 31 ton smack *Myra* in 1832. There were also Simons associated with shipping in Aberdyfi.

Some families moved from place to place following maritime employment opportunities along the west Wales seaboard. There were seafaring Daniels in Borth for most of the 19th century, beginning with Thomas Daniel, born in 1774 who was associated with the sloop *Amity* in 1799 and the Borth schooner *Francis* in 1824. His son David Daniel born in 1805 was master of the sloops *Dove* and *Linnet*. Captain Aiden Daniel commanded the schooner *Aquila* in 1834. Were these Borth Daniels related to the Daniels involved with Aberdyfi shipping, especially the brig *Charlotte*? Another Borth to Aberdyfi movement was by members of the Morgan and Davies families, which is well documented in *Brief Glory* by their descendant D.W. Morgan. Members of another Davies family that feature in the photograph around the *Neena*, moved southward to Aberystwyth. Their descendant Desmond Davies, had a long career at sea, primarily in ships captained by Borth men. Another southward movement was by the Jenkins family. Captain David Jenkins, born in 1840, lived at Portland Road, Aberystwyth. He commanded several ships and drowned on the *Hope* in 1892. His brother, Captain Evan Jenkins, born 1841, lived at Havelock Villa, on Penglais Hill. The house was named after one of the ships that he owned and commanded in the 1880s, the *Lady Havelock*. The Richards brothers, Ted and Jac, always maintained that Captain David Richards of the schooner

Maglona, was a close relative of their grandfather, Captain William Richards (pers. comm, 1970). The Maglona and its master have appeared as part of Aberdyfi's history... curiously there was a Maglona House in Borth in the 1870s. The schooner was lost at Cape Race, Newfoundland in 1887 whilst seeking a cargo of salt cod.

Eminent and respectable though the Borth captains were thought to be, especially in retirement, there were some scallywags who realised that the captains' vanity could be their undoing. This led to a very elaborate series of practical jokes devised by some of the local seamen. The headquarters of the plotters was the Victoria Inn near one venerable Master Mariner's home. A letter was written by the one with the most decent handwriting purporting to come from a comely Aberdyfi widow, anonymously of course. It was an effusive and gushing letter saying how much she admired the captain and felt that despite her shyness, they should meet. In the letter's besotted praise for the 'old salt' was a passage that appealed to his 'Cardi' instincts. It was a thinly veiled reference to the fact that she was financially well off. To add authenticity, perfume was sprinkled on the letter before it was given to one of the conspirators' relatives to post from Machynlleth on his way to Liverpool. The letter included a date for a meeting at Glandyfi junction. The writer had also included a description of herself as being a lady with a fulsome figure and wearing a rose in her hat. Part of the plan for proposed rendezvous was that they would travel back together to Aberdyfi for tea.

At the appointed hour the pranksters waited in the pub to see if the captain had 'taken the bait' and behold, half an hour before the midday train was to leave Borth, out of the house stepped the captain in all his finery. His shirt was gleaming white and in the bright spring sunlight the braid and brass was dazzling. Sporting a silver topped cane and clutching a bunch of flowers, he set off with a decided swagger toward Borth station. Previously wary boys and cats were unexpectedly given a friendly pat and cheery greetings were surprisingly extended to all those he passed. This striking appearance of the captain left Borth in good humour. Hours later, a flustered, black browed captain returned and kicked cats and cuffed boys as he stalked back to his house. The revellers in the tavern were in stitches. This practical joke was continued when another letter soon arrived at the captain's home, written by the same hand begging his forgiveness and pleading that a bout of nerves and modesty had led her to have cold feet at the last minute she stated that she had in fact stayed on the train until it got to Machynlleth. The mystery lady from Aberdyfi now arranged another meeting. This happened three times before 'the penny dropped'. This trick was played on several susceptible captains, because the pranksters realised that embarrassment prevented the captains discussing it with anyone. The storyteller and plotter Gwilym Davies, said "they must have gone to their graves half believing that a rich plump widow had once been within their grasp"(G. Davies, pers. comm. 1964).

A large number of Borth master mariners, many of whom had started in sail during the height of Aberdyfi's slate export boom, finished their careers in steam ships. Their retirement in the first quarter of the 20th century heralded a flurry of house building at both ends of the village. The first houses on the cliff were built by sea captains, beginning with Captain William Richards' houses the two Maelgwyns in 1904. Later Bay Ridge was built by Captain Davies, who had a notoriously rude parrot which verbally abused any visitors knocking on the door. Then came Francon built by Captain Williams who carried horses from the Argentine to supply the army's needs during World War 1. The nearby St Albans houses were likewise financed by shipping enterprise. The row of large houses currently being renovated at the northern end of Borth, including Montford and Ballarat were also built by sea captains. Surrey, Glendower and Maesarfor were associated with the maritime Jones family, whose descendant David Jones now lives at Ynyslas. One of this family, Captain Jones, appears in a photograph, *Borth Captains*, circa 1910. To date, only he and Captain William Richards have been identified amongst this particular group of sitters.

Captain Richards was based in Mostyn, the port of Chester, during the latter half of his career, and was involved with two steamships the *S.S. Eira* and *S.S.Lady Mostyn*. He took his wife on several trips on these vessels. Unfortunately both vessels were lost, but Captain Richards was not on either of them when tragedies occurred. The *Eira* was lost with all hands after departing on a voyage from Whitehaven to Kronstad on the 13th October 1898. The *Lady Mostyn* foundered in the Pentland Firth carrying railway lines to the Estonian port of Riga in the Baltic. Captain Richards was a pretty tough customer but had a sense of humour. On one voyage, three of his Borth crew members found themselves in jail in a French port for drunken behavior in a house of disrepute. The captain was summoned by an officious Frenchman to come and redeem them for a certain fee. Richards took one look at the now contrite crew members and announced "pydrwch y diawled", (rot you devils), and stalked out. The French official was told in no uncertain terms by the captain that he wouldn't get any bribe money and the authorities could damn well feed and water the men until he returned in a couple of months' time (J. Richards, pers. comm. 1970).

On arriving back in a British port one of the first things Captain Richards wanted was an English newspaper. When it arrived, the other officers, also eager for news, began the habit of reading over his shoulder. Fed up with this, the captain would turn the newspaper upside down and pretend to read it. In the end the over-shoulder readers cracked and asked him why the newspaper was upside down? He unhesitatingly replied, "Any fool can read it the right way up". He gleefully continued this practice whenever others were present. Newspapers proved vexatious things, even in the captain's retirement. He was quite adamant about receiving the *Cambrian News* well before his daughter Elizabeth got hold of it. Elizabeth Richards was a member of the Emmeline Pankhurst circle of suffragettes and, according to Tom Macdonald, in his memoirs entitled *The White Lanes of Summer*, would cause quite a stir in the villages of Bow Street and Pengarn on her frequent visits home from London. Not only was she attractive, dressed in the high style of the day, but she smoked in public! If she got hold of the *Cambrian News* before her father it would become unreadable, as she was unable to judge the distance of the cigarette on the end of a foot long holder. This resulted in the newspaper being covered in brown and black spots which, rendered it illegible.

Will John 'Science' was a regular Borth crew member on Richards's ships. William John Hughes's nickname 'Science' was given to him because of a physical affliction that saw him walk in an exaggerated manner. The term 'science' was used when describing an over elaboration of manner or behavior. John Hughes of Caenant, tells a story of David John Richards who rode a bicycle all the way down the many steep entrance steps of the now demolished Pantyfedwen. When asked how he managed this extraordinary feat he replied "by science" and thereafter he was known as David John "Science" (J. Hughes, pers. comm. 2003). John Hughes's antecedents were major players in Borth's shipping as far back as the 18th century.

Will John "Science's" usual job was of cook, and part of his duties was to keep the captain's quarters clean. On his first voyage in this post Will John decided that he would, for the sake of economy, use the dishwater to mop out the captain's quarters. For this he received a clout and was told to mop the vessel from stem to stern with clean water. From there on in there was no further acrimony between these two as Will John Hughes was for years a regular crew member. He is depicted wearing an apron, standing behind the bowler hatted Captain Richards in the *Eira* crew photograph. Thomas Hughes, a relative of Will John, was first mate under Captain Williams of Aberystwyth at the time of the sinking of the *Eira*, which claimed another Borth man Henry Jones, Thomas Hughes' brother-in-law. Although a relief fund was set up, apparently not a penny was received by the Borth victims' relatives (N.Sharpe, pers. comm. 2003).

The other side of Captain William Richards's nature saw him take care of a storm-battered seagull which had landed on board his ship to seek out scraps. He mended its badly broken leg with delicate splints until it was fit to fly off. His fondness for birds saw him continually bring home exotic parrots. The birds would escape and land in local farmyards to feed with the chickens, causing a great hullabaloo as the poultry were frightened of these strange relatives and no doubt the farmers were equally startled. It was the captain's son's unenviable task to retrieve the birds and calm down all concerned. He was often abused in the process. The captain once brought home a mongoose, whose fate has always been a mystery. Did it escape to be shot by locals who thought it was a polecat… or was its demise engineered by the exasperated son?

Captain Richards retired inland to another of his houses, again named Maelgwyn, where he took up gardening in a serious way. He planted an orchard and had a heated glass house producing some of the first tomatoes grown in the area. The old seafarer's one concession to his former career was a private study planked out to resemble a ship's cabin. In the '*The White Lanes of Summer*', Captain Richards, who is described as having "far seeing blue eyes", is mentioned frequently, and one passage refers to him conversing fluently with an itinerant Italian tramp. Strange to think that with his fluency in Italian he should complain about the difficulties of sitting his Masters' Examination when he declared; "it wasn't the complex mathematics or navigational issues that I found hard, but that it, was all in English". It was this remark that made me consider that the woman in the photograph '*Borth Captains and Lady*', was coaching the mariners in the intricacies of the English language.

As builder of the first two houses on the cliff on Pengoitan Farm's land, he decided that the stone for the front should come from a cliff top location near Brynbala farmhouse where relatives of his lived. Today, on the cliff-top walk between Borth and Wallog one can still see the remains of the little quarry. In true Richards style, he organised transportation of the stone to the Borth site. After quarrying, the stones were roughly dressed on the cliff top and tossed down the cliff face to the beach far below. A swch (barge), was constructed and floated on the high tide over the rock shelf to the waiting dressed stone deposit. Whilst the tide was out, the stones were loaded onto the barge which later moved off with the returning sea. It was towed by another boat using a sail and four oarsmen to help take advantage of the tide flowing northwards towards Borth. It was bought inside Trwyn Cyntaf to the small indent in the low cliffs opposite the building site. To hoist the stones up the cliff face, the captain organised a swivelling two pole gantry so that when the load of stone got to the block at the apex of the gantry it was pulled in and the gantry came with it, depositing the stone onto the cliff top. Captain Richards was always adept at practical solutions, and once in Bergen harbour his quick thinking prevented a Swedish ship from breaking apart and depositing her cargo into the harbour. He organised chains to be bound around the vessel whilst the crew carefully and quickly unloaded the cargo. He was handsomely rewarded by the ship's insurer for averting a costly disaster. Every two years, he would receive a bonus from his own ship's insurers for avoiding accidents… a kind of maritime no-claim bonus.

Many others also took advantage of the tidal flow to haul rafts of salvaged timber back to Borth from Traeth Bach near Wallog. In Borth, usable timber washed ashore was called 'sprokes', which probably came from the word strakes. The main ceiling beam in the now demolished Felin Wern farmhouse was a ship's mast (Dilwyn Owen, pers. comm. 1970). Considering the age of the building, one wonders if it was from the 1732 Portuguese wreck. There is a story of a local cobbler, who having run out of leather decided one summer's day to take advantage of the tidal flow and row south with the ebb to Aberystwyth to replenish supplies. To finance this venture he took most of the much needed household budget. Arriving in Aberystwyth hot and sweating after his exertions, he decided to quench his thirst at a local inn; this was to be his undoing. On the long row back, serried ranks of seagulls on the cliff face were the audience for a medley of Welsh hymns sung uninhibitedly by the merry cobbler. Hours later rounding Trwyn Pellaf on the incoming tide, he could be heard singing R.S.Hughes's song *Arafa Don* (Slow Thou Wave). His wife, who was down on the beach to help pull the boat up, realised that about to disembark was one drunken cobbler with no money or leather, so she brought an abrupt end to the cobbler's serenading. He was firmly boxed around the ears and from then on his wife walked to Aberystwyth to ensure a supply of shoe leather.

In addition to mariners, some of Borth's other tradesmen were attracted to the growing prosperity of Aberdyfi. Blacksmith John Jenkins of Borth moved to Aberdyfi in 1859 where the demand for anchors, chains and other metal parts for shipbuilding was increasing. Amongst the parents of the first pupils of Borth's Morfa School when it opened in 1842, were five blacksmiths (Enoch, 2002, p.71). Although this does not tally with the 1841 census which records Borth as having only one; the explanation lies in the fact that the five smithies were drawn from the greater Borth area. As well as John Jenkins who moved across the Dyfi, there was John Richards at Rhydmeirionydd, the brothers Lewis and Richard Jones in Penybont, Hugh Williams at Gwastad and John Richard of Borth. Today's Evelwen (White Smithy) must have been a working forge at one time, but there is no record to date of a blacksmith residing in Morfa Borth. Evelwen as far back as 1840 was the joinery workshop of Evan Griffith and upon his retirement in 1880 his son-in-law, carpenter John Beynon, took over. The previously mentioned blacksmith, Hugh Williams of Gwastad, was a renowned poacher. Gogerddan gamekeepers were continually frustrated as they tried every trick in the book to catch him redhanded. He had an uncanny knack of sensing danger and he would often leave his gun and catch hidden in hedges on his way back to Gwastad as he knew the gamekeepers would often be waiting to ambush him. Other favoured hiding places were numerous neighbours' haystacks or lofts (David Griffiths, pers. comm. 1970).

In rural Welsh communities wisdom was usually disseminated in the various craft workshops of smithy, carpenter or cobbler. In Borth, this wisdom was mainly within the province of sea captains, as after all they were the village's main employers and provided the only investment opportunity. To achieve this they obviously had to be worldly wise and shrewd in their business dealings. However, there were others who were viewed as sages, such as John Beynon, who in the last quarter of the 19th century played a major role in constructing the first large-scale sea defence system in Borth. The Rev. J. James of Brynllys was also held in high regard. He was a deeply religious, kindly man who was adept at bone setting and provided herbal medicines that, like his advice, were free of charge. William Jones professed to cure many ailments by using wool as a healing medium, a common practice in Wales. He would bind various parts of the body with woollen twine or cloths which he would remove and rebind until the patient was cured. Many of my generation suffered the indignity of having to wear a piece of woollen cloth next to our chest to ward off colds in the winter time, probably a direct descendant of the wool cure-all! William Jones lived near today's Craigfryn in the ruined cottage whose gable end remains can be seen in the old photograph of Borth taken near the slip.

There were also some who were apparently involved in the darker arts which were still practiced even in my childhood. I grew up in a world where the Welsh word 'rheibo', to curse, was in common use. I notice that a Mr Pryse of Ffos-y-grafel gave generously to the Llandre church's one million pound fund, with a contribution of £100 (Enoch, 2002, p.147). He must have been having an 'each way bet' as he is the feared conjurer mentioned in *The White Lanes of Summer*, where it records that when his coffin was lowered into the grave, hordes of black goblins escaped (Macdonald, 1975, p.69). The present owner of Ffos-y-grafel, Mr Iorwerth Mason, related that Mr Pryse built the farmhouse with very high ceilings to accommodate a tall lady whom he intended to marry. Alas, it was not to be, and as Mr Mason wryly observed, "despite a fearsome reputation he wasn't much of a conjurer after all" (I. Mason, pers. comm. 1999). Even an Enlightenment sophisticate like Lewis Morris believed in 'knockers', which were supposed to be beings who lived in the earth and caused knocking sounds often heard in the lead mines of Ceredigion.

There were three Borth master mariners all named David Davies. One was known as Captain Davies, Glanwern, born 1838, who lived in Glanwern House and was the skipper and principal owner of the schooner *Cecil Brindley*. He co-owned this vessel with Borth man John Francis. This vessel had strong associations with the village as it had been another Borth man, William Richards's first command in 1873. Another Captain David Davies born in 1854 began his career at 14, and by the time he was 18 was A.B. on the schooner *Beatrice*. He was lost in 1892 in a massive storm with all the crew whilst in command of the *Eleanor and Jane*, a West country-built schooner which he also owned. The third moved to Aberdyfi around 1875 after marrying Margaret, his first wife. This David Davies, born on the 7th of May, 1848, was one of four children of mariner John Davies and his wife Mary, formerly Jenkins. Two of his brothers William and Thomas had connections with the sea and lived in Barry; the third, Lewis, lived in Taliesin. Captain Davies began his long maritime career at 14 years of age on the schooners *Sarah, Jane Sophia* and the *Frances Poole*. He was soon a first mate on deepwater sailing ships, which meant his navigational skills were outstanding. It was from the 1,065 ton barque, *Snowdon*, whose commander was Borth master mariner John Lewis, that David Davies went to Hull in 1882 to sit his master's examination and on the 23rd May was granted his Master Mariner's Certificate, no.93613. His global voyages took him around the Horn to the west coast of South America as well as to Bangkok, Argentina, India, Java, Brazil and the West Indies. In 1887, he was master of the schooner *Sarah Davies*. Despite having a Master's Certificate he mainly served as first mate which was the usual practice when there was no command position available; such an experience was recalled in the memoirs of Captain Davies of Maesteg House.

Certificates of discharge chart much of Captain David Davies's career, but at present little is known of other ships he may have captained. He had connections with Borth master mariner William Richards voyaging with him on the *S.S. Lady Mostyn* in 1884. Many of his discharge papers and letters of recommendation have survived, as has a portrait of him and a model of a fully rigged ship named after his first wife, Margaret, formerly Gray-Jones. In light of his association with the aforementioned Captain Richards, and the existence of this fine painting, it is easy to identify him as the first mate in the crew photograph of the *S.S. Eira* taken in 1884. Captain Davies also appears in a photograph of Borth skippers. In a long career he alternated with seeming ease between sailing ships and steamers. Some of the sailing ships he served on were *Acorn, Margaret Lewis, Rowland Evans, Clara, Lord Tredegar, Granville, Snowdon, Emily A Davies, Zimi, Iolo, Ivanhoe* and *Coromandel*, and he served on the steamers *Lady Mostyn, Eira, Harkaway, James Wishaw, Manchester* and *Iolo Morganwg*. Like so many others he learnt his sea-going skills during childhood sailing Borth waters chasing the herring.

As well as captains there were also ships bearing the same name. There were three Borth vessels with the name *Picton*, a sloop in 1824, a smack in 1832 and a schooner in 1839. According to Miss Davies of Angorfa House, there was apparently another schooner called *Picton Castle* that had connections with the Hughes family of Castle Stores. Prior to the

Hughes's association with this property, Captain Hugh James lived at No 2, Picton Terrace, Upper Borth, in the late 1870s, when there were two dwellings at the site of today's Castle Stores. The name Picton moved northwards from here to today's Arfor for a time, and then on to its current location. (Teddy Davies, pers. comm. 2003). There were also two *John Wesleys*, one a fishing boat, the other a schooner and two *Pilgrims*, one a brig and the other a schooner. Occasionally a sloop's name was used again when the owners acquired a schooner, an example of this is *Francis*, and also *Britannia*. Captain John Davies, born 1850, of the schooner *Pilgrim,* lived at today's Holmleigh, next door to the then, 1 London Place, now known as Nerella, where there was a murder in 1894. During an attempted theft, seaman Thomas Richards, a distant relative of Captain William Richards, murdered Mary Davies, wife of mariner James Davies. The offender Thomas Richards, had sailed as a 19 year old crew member on *the Cecil Brindley* with Captain Richards in 1873. It is believed that the murder took place upstairs in the northern end bedroom. Thomas Richards was hanged in Carmarthen and his 38 year old victim buried in Pengarn cemetry (A. Budge, pers. comm. 2003).

Often, local boys as young as eight went to sea. This was the age that the uncles of Captain John Davies of Maesteg house began their maritime careers. No wonder they became master mariners by the time they were 24, as by then they had had fourteen years seagoing experience. Such were the risks of seafaring that three of the aforementioned uncles had lost their lives by the time they were 30. In his memoirs Captain Davies tells us of the quirky coincidence where both he and his father had the same skipper on their respective maiden voyages; namely Captain Richard Jenkins who was still commanding ships at the age of 75. In his youth, Captain Davies had served under sail with Captain Evan Lewis Davies of Borth on the barque Zinnia, and went on to have a remarkable career during which he became a ship owner. From 1917 to 1937 he owned schooners and steamers. He 'tramped' all over the world and was fondly known as John 'China', as he had captained the *Klukiang*, and the *Foochow* (H.Hughes, pers.comm. 2003). One of Captain Davies's schooners the *Brandon,* was sunk by enemy fire in 1918, and another schooner the *Industry*, still working well into the 20th century, was wrecked in 1921 on the Irish coast. From that time on he concentrated on steamers such as the *Plas Dinam* of Aberystwyth.

Some ship's captains resided in the outlying areas of Borth. Captain Richard Edwards and Captain David Davies lived at Glanwern as did the Lloyd family of mariners of Cwmcethin House who are the antecedents of Gwen and Derek Lloyd. Captain Daniel of Pengraig Farm owned the first Borth schooner, the *Francis;* Captain Thomas Jones of Ffos y Gravel Farm owned and captained the brig *Pilgrim* and Captain Hugh Hughes of Tynparc was associated with the sloop *The Dart*. Of the 142 mariners who were members of the Castell Gwallter Ivorites 97 were from Morfa Borth, 20 from Borth, 3 from Gwastad Y Borth, 3 from Penybont, 3 from Glanwern, 2 from Dolybont and 2 from Henllys Farm. William James and his brother, Enoch, were both master mariners, and lived at Henllys in the early 1870s. The James family eventually moved to Aberdyfi and were involved with the *Ocean Belle, Dorothy, Island Maid* and the *Glendovey*; interestingly their successor at Henllys Farm, Richard Watkin Smith had shares in the *Glendovey* in 1878.

The surrounding villages of Llandre, Talybont, Taliesin and Tre'r-ddôl also had ship's captains. One was Captain Griffiths who was the grandfather of today's Mrs Davies of Dolclettwr Hall Farm. He was born in Dolau of farming stock, and at fourteen had to leave home to make his own way. He went out into the world to work for the vicar of Pennal with only the half a crown his widowed mother had given him. He had not been at the post long when he demonstrated his mettle by refusing to carry firewood into the vicarage on a Sunday. His employer quickly realised that young Griffiths was intelligent and had great potential. Having recognised his penchant for seafaring, his ecclesiastical mentor sent him to learn navigation with Cranogwen at Llangrannog, south Ceredigion. He eventually gained his Master Mariner's Certificate in Dublin and commanded the Roebuck and *The Mexican*. On one of his voyages, after a two year absence it was presumed that the ship and crew were lost. No sooner had the insurance been paid out and all other matters settled, than the long overdue ship returned causing great consternation. Apparently after this event Captain Griffiths gave up seafaring to concentrate on farming at Dolclettwr (pers. comm. Davies, 2003).

Mrs Davies of Dolcletwr Farm's great aunt Anne also married a sea captain, Captain William Richards of Borth. Obviously sea captains were quite a catch, but often the uncertain fate of a seafarer's life intervened. Amongst many tales of loss and ensuing hardship is the case of Captain David Rees and his wife Elizabeth. In 1879 they became the proud owners of the barque *Drusus*. This vessel had been built in Sunderland in 1857 and had a male figurehead depicting a Roman noble. An artist was commissioned to paint her so she could be displayed proudly on the wall of Gloucester House. Two years later, Captain Rees died and his widow Elizabeth tried to continue with their investment, but after another two years the vessel had to be sold. From that time there is no further mention of the human players in this drama, nor is there at present any documentation as to the subsequent fate of the vessel. Luckily, Hugh Hughes, a descendant of the Rees family on his mother's side, has the painting of this beautiful ship which appears on the cover of this book.

46. Captain David Davies repairing boat

47. Seamans Delight

48. Captain William Richards and family, circa 1890

49. Borth captains, circa 1890

50. Borth captains, circa 1890, with the names of their ships. Back row left to right: H. Hughes The Dart, J. Evans Savatele, W. Jones Picton, R. Jones Charlotte, J. Hughes Lorne, David Rees Sabrina, John Francis Eleanor Francis. Front row: D. Hughes Friendship, John Hughes Jane Martha, John Edwards Reform, T. Davies Venus, William Jones Panthea and John Richards Catherine.

51. Borth Captains and Lady, circa 1890

52. Borth Captains, circa 1910

53. Native Captains Borth, circa 1900

54. Captains Thomas Davies and John Jones

55. Crew of the Eira, *1888*

56. Crew of the Glanhafren, *1894*

BORTH CAPTAINS & THEIR SHIPS

Below is a list of sailing ships of various kinds. Though only some were owned by Borth inhabitants all were skippered at one time by Borth masters. Some of the vessels listed appear several times with different Borth masters and vice versa. The prime source is the Aberystwyth Port books which unfortunately exclude the first volumes which would have covered the period from 1780 to 1824. There were also many locally owned ships registered elsewhere which makes the task of a comprehensive list at this time difficult. An example is the schooner *Pluvier* 1892, master and owner Thomas Davies of Borth, which was registered at Plymouth where she was built.

Sloops were the preferred commercial vessels up until the 1840s. From then on until the beginning of the 20th century, schooners became the first choice, to such a degree that sloops ceased to be built in the Dyfi area after the 1860s. There were also some locally owned brigs, snows and barques. The latter, because of their size had to be based elsewhere. By the 1890's the once substantial local schooner fleet was rapidly dwindling, and with it Borth residents' involvement as owners. Increasingly, larger sailing vessels, by then competing with steam, were now owned by companies operating from Britain's major ports. The inevitable triumph of steam over sail meant that many areas of the Welsh coastline that had previously flourished in the days of sail now withered. This factor, coupled with the impact of the increasingly proficient railway freight system, ushered in the collapse of Ceredigion's shipping industry.

The second entry in the list below is the sloop *Providence*, which was half owned by a Jaen (Jane?) Hugh of Borth. In her will of 1786 she left her share to John Rees, the regular skipper, asking him, in his new capacity as owner, to make an honest covenant with the other owner Thomas Pryse (Manuscript SD1786/124, N.L.W.). There are records of older wills in the Borth area, dating back to the early 1600's, which mention amongst the bequests, shares in boats and nets.

My research to date indicates that there were approximately 160 Master Mariners from Borth... there may be more. Many of the persons named in the following list were Master Mariners. The dates on the right hand column are of the vessel's registration or the year in which a Borth captain commanded the listed vessel.

LINNET	Sloop	John Jones	1769
PROVIDENCE	Sloop	John Rees	1774
BEE	Sloop	John Thomas	1783
FRIENDSHIP	Sloop	David Hughes the elder	1788
BOTALOG	Sloop	David Morgan	1788
HOPEWELL	Sloop	Hugh Humphries	1789
AMITY	Sloop	Thomas Daniel	1799
SINCERITY	Sloop	Rees Lewis	1803
MARY & ANN	Sloop	Thomas Daniel	1812

MARINER	Sloop	Hugh Hughes	1815
PICTON	Sloop	John Davies the elder	1824
NEPTUNE	Sloop	John Jones	1824
CAMBRIA	Sloop	Thomas Thomas	1824
FRIENDSHIP	Sloop	John Hughes	1824
FRANCIS	Schooner	Thomas Daniel	1824
MARY	Sloop	Hugh Davies	1824
BETSEY	Sloop	John Williams	1824
SPEEDWELL	Sloop	William Morgan	1825
AID	Sloop	Enoch James	1825
GLEANOR	Sloop	Richard Edwards	1825
ANNE & BETSY	Sloop	Richard Watkins	1825
FAME	Sloop	John Morgan	1825
HOPE	Sloop	David Hughes the elder	1825
LIVERPOOL TRADER	Sloop	Evan Hughes	1825
ELEANOR	Sloop	Richard Edwards	1825
AMITY	Sloop	John Davies the elder	1825
PROVIDENCE	Sloop	Thomas Rees	1826
PEGGY	Sloop	John Lewis	1826
NEW GIFT	Sloop	John Hughes	1826
BRITANNIA	Sloop	Richard Jones	1826
SUCCESS	Sloop	Thomas Thomas	1826
VENUS	Sloop	John Davies the elder	1826
LINNET	Sloop	Morgan Jones	1826
SINCERITY	Sloop	Hugh Jones	1826
CAMBRIA	Sloop	John Williams	1826
AMITY	Sloop	John Edwards	1826
BETSEY	Sloop	David Hughes	1826
ACTIVE	Sloop	Evan Thomas	1827
MARY	Sloop	Evan Hughes	1827
BETSEY	Sloop	John Morgan	1827
ENDEAVOUR	Sloop	John Davies the elder	1828
PROVIDENCE	Sloop	John Williams	1828
FRANCE	Sloop	Lewis Morgan	1828
VICTORY	Sloop	Hugh Jones	1829
SUSANNA & MARY	Sloop	Richard Davies	1830
WONDER	Sloop	Thomas Thomas	1830

ELEANOR & BETTY	Smack	David Morgan	1831
DOVE	Sloop	William Morgan	1831
ROBUST	Sloop	John Simon the elder	1832
SWALLOW	Smack	John Jones	1832
REFORM	Schooner	John Edwards	1832
PICTON	Smack	Richard Jones	1832
MARGARET	Sloop	Evan Hughes	1833
AQUILA	Schooner	Aiden Daniel	1834
MARY	Sloop	John Davies	1834
BEE	Sloop	William Williams	1834
ACTIVE	Sloop	John Hughes	1835
HOPE	Sloop	David Hughes	1836
VICTORY	Sloop	Thomas Williams	1836
ELEANOR & BETSEY	Sloop	William Morgan	1836
MERMAID	Sloop	John Evans	1836
MARGARET	Sloop	Evan Hughes	1836
PERSEVERANCE	Sloop	David James	1836
AID	Sloop	Enoch James	1836
DOVE	Sloop	David Daniel	1836
VENUS	Sloop	Abraham Davies	1837
NEW GIFT	Sloop	John Hughes	1837
NEPTUNE	Sloop	Evan Hughes	1837
LIVERPOOL TRADER	Sloop	John Rees	1837
FRIENDSHIP	Sloop	Evan Hughes	1837
ANNA	Sloop	William Williams	1837
SARAH	Flat	William J Davies	1837
FRANCES	Schooner	Hugh Davies	1837
ENDEAVOUR	Sloop	John Davies the younger	1838
FRANCES	Sloop	Lewis Morgan	1838
FANCY	Sloop	Evan Williams	1838
LINNET	Sloop	William Francis	1838
AMITY	Sloop	John Davies	1838
SWALLOW	Sloop	William Jones	1838
PROVIDENCE	Sloop	Evan Hughes	1838
LINNET	Sloop	David Daniel	1838
UNITY	Sloop	Richard Edwards	1839
PROVIDENCE (b. Garreg)	Sloop	John Rees	1839

SWAN	Sloop	David Thomas	1839
PROVIDENCE (b. Barmouth)	Sloop	John Williams	1839
LAURA & ELIZABETH	Schooner	John Evans	1839
PROVIDENCE	Sloop	Evan Jenkins	1839
MARY ANN	Sloop	Richard Jones	1839
BROTHERS	Sloop	Evan Hughes	1840
ELEANOR	Sloop	David Thomas	1840
AQUILA	Schooner	David Davies the younger	1840
BRITANNIA	Schooner	Richard Jones	1840
SUCCESS	Schooner	Lewis Jones	1840
HOPE	Sloop	Richard Davies	1840
SPEEDWELL	Schooner	John Lewis	1841
BOTALOG	Schooner	William Morgan	1841
DOVE	Schooner	John Morgan	1841
ELEANOR	Schooner	David Thomas	1841
VICTORY	Schooner	Thomas Williams	1841
JOHN & MARY	Sloop	John Hughes	1842
MARGARET MARY	Smack	Richard Jones	1842
MARY & ELLEN	Sloop	Enoch Jones	1842
MARY REES	Sloop	John Rees	1842
CATHERINE & ELLEN	Schooner	David Hughes	1842
SWALLOW	Sloop	William Jones	1842
FRIENDSHIP	Sloop	Evan Hughes	1842
ELEANOR	Sloop	David Thomas	1842
FRIENDSHIP	Sloop	David Hughes	1842
MARGARET	Sloop	John Jones	1844
VENUS	Sloop	Thomas Davies	1844
EAGLE	Sloop	John Richards	1845
CATERINA	Sloop	John Morgan	1845
THOMAS	Sloop	Evan Hughes	1845
LAURA & ELIZABETH	Schooner	John Jones	1845
HOPEWELL	Sloop	Thomas Jones	1845
MERMAID	Sloop	William Williams	1845
COUNTESS OF LISBURNE	Smack	John Williams	1845
FRIENDSHIP	Sloop	John Arter	1846
MARGARET MARY	Smack	Enoch Jones the younger	1846
ANNE JONES	Schooner	William Williams	1847

OSPREY	Sloop	David Jenkins	1847
VENUS	Sloop	Thomas Davies	1847
FRIENDS	Sloop	David Davies	1847
AMITY	Sloop	John Davies	1847
EMMET	Schooner	William Jones	1848
FRIENDSHIP (Fach)	Sloop	William Jones	1848
MARY & ELLEN	Schooner	John Jones	1848
LIVELY	Sloop	John Hughes	1848
OCEAN	Schooner	John Lewis	1848
VIRTUE	Sloop	John Hughes	1848
FAVOURITE	Sloop	Evan Williams	1848
ANNE & MARY	Sloop	William Williams	1848
GLEANOR	Schooner	David Jones	1848
SWALLOW	Sloop	John Griffiths	1848
BEST	Schooner	James Evans	1848
FRIENDS	Sloop	David Davies	1848
HOPE	Sloop	William Williams	1849
PICTON	Schooner	William Jones	1849
RESOLUTE	Schooner	Richard James	1849
CLAUDIA	Smack	William Francis	1849
ISLAND MAID	Brigantine	William Jones	1849
CLARA	Smack	Evan Hughes	1849
AMITY	Sloop	David Davies	1849
BROTHERS	Smack	David Hughes	1849
MARY ANN	Sloop	William Morris	1849
AQUILA	Schooner	John Hughes	1849
HOPE	Schooner	John Jenkins	1850
SARAH & MARY	Schooner	John Evans the younger	1852
CLARA	Sloop	Evan Hughes	1852
DILIGENCE	Smack	Richard Edwards	1853
AQUILA	Schooner	Enoch Jones	1854
KING OF THE FOREST	Schooner	John Hughes	1854
ADELAIDE	Schooner	John Simon	1854
ROSINA	Schooner	James Watkin Davies	1854
FRANCIS	Smack	David Morgan	1855
EMMET	Sloop	Lewis Jones	1855
PRISCILLA	Sloop	Evan Jenkins	1855

FALCON	Schooner	John Rees	1857
MARY ANNE	Brigantine	John Jenkins	1857
CATHERINE	Sloop	David Hughes	1857
JANE JONES	Schooner	John Jones	1857
JANE & MARY	Schooner	Evan Hughes	1857
PANTHEA	Barque	William Jones	1858
SARAH	Schooner	John Evans	1858
AMITY	Sloop	John Griffiths	1858
BEATRICE	Schooner	Enoch James	1858
SWANSEA TRADER	Smack	David Jenkins	1858
ELEANOR FRANCIS	Schooner	John Francis	1858
JANE ELLEN	Schooner	Hugh Morgan	1858
CERES	Schooner	David Richards	1858
CATHERINE MORGAN	Schooner	John Jones	1858
MARTHA LLOYD	Schooner	David Lloyd	1858
FRANCIS POOLE	Schooner	William Lewis	1858
ELIZABETH & MARGARET	Smack	David Williams	1863
JANE SOPHIA	Schooner	John Lewis	1863
MARTHA LLOYD	Schooner	Abraham Lloyd	1863
OCEAN BELLE	Snow	John Williams	1863
JANE OWENS	Schooner	Thomas Lewis	1863
ACORN	Schooner	John Rees	1864
MARY LEWIS	Schooner	Hugh Jones	1864
JANE OWENS	Schooner	John Davies	1864
ELEANOR & BETSEY	Smack	Hugh Morgan	1864
CATHERINE	Smack	Hugh Hughes	1864
MORRISTON	Smack	Thomas Davies	1864
JULIETTE	Sloop	John Jones	1864
ROWLAND EVANS	Brig	John Evans	1864
XANTHUS	Brigantine	Hugh Morgan	1864
JANE MARTHA	Barque	John Hughes	1865
GLAD TIDINGS	Schooner	John Jenkins	1865
NAOMI	Brig	David Lloyd	1865
REBECCA	Brigantine	David Rees	1865
FALCON	Schooner	John Lewis	1865
MORBEN	Smack	John Jenkins	1865
MIDAS	Sloop	David Davies	1866

AZOFF	Schooner	Hugh Jones	1866
GRATITUDE	Schooner	Richard Jones	1866
JANE SOPHIA	Schooner	James Morgans	1866
MARY EVANS	Barque	John Davies	1868
JOHN WESLEY	Schooner	James Morgan	1868
ALERT	Sloop	Richard Jenkins	1868
KOH-I-NOOR	Schooner	John Hughes	1869
DOVEY BELLE	Schooner	John James	1869
LIZZIE JANE	Schooner	John Hughes	1869
ALICE	Barque	John Jones	1869
JANE SOPHIA	Schooner	John Lewis	1870
LADY OF THE FOREST	Schooner	John Jenkins	1870
DOROTHY	Barque	Lewis Jenkins	1870
SEVEN BROTHERS	Schooner	James Morgan	1870
IVANHOE	Barque	David Hughes	1871
JULETTE	Barque	Richard Davies	1872
SAVATELE	Schooner	John Evans	1872
MARGARET LEWIS	Schooner	John Lewis	1873
CHARLOTTE	Brigantine	Richard Jones	1873
CECIL BRINDLEY	Schooner	William Richards	1873
CATHERINE	Schooner	John Richards	1873
CAMBRIAN	Schooner	Thomas Lewis	1873
MARGARET LEWIS	Schooner	John Lewis	1873
SOPHIE & EMILY	Schooner	David Jenkins	1873
COURIER	Brig	John Francis	1874
ELIZABETH THOMAS	Schooner	Richard Jones	1874
CAMBRIAN	Schooner	William Arter	1874
FALCON	Schooner	Enoch James	1874
GLENALVON	Barque	Thomas Lewis	1874
LORNE	Schooner	John Hughes	1875
SOLWAY	Brig	Richard Davies	1875
LADY ZETLAND	Schooner	Hugh Hughes	1875
DOROTHY	Barque	John Williams	1876
CLARA	Brigantine	John Williams	1876
ROSEDALE	Barque	Peter Rowlands	1877
GRANVILLE	Barque	John Williams	1878
ELIZABETH & MARGARET	Smack	Thomas Williams	1878

CAROLINE SPOONER	Barque	John Hughes	1878
SWALLOW	Schooner	William Williams	1878
NERISSA	Schooner	David Jenkins	1878
ELEANOR & THOMAS	Schooner	John Lloyd	1878
DRUSUS	Barque	David Rees	1879
BERTIE	Barque	David Daniel	1879
MAGLONA	Schooner	David Richards	1879
MEIRION LASS	Schooner	James Morgan	1880
GLENDOVEY	Barque	John Williams	1880
EOS	Barque	John Enos	1880
EURYDICE	Barque	Edward Edwards	1880
OLIVE BRANCH	Schooner	John Davies	1880
SABRINA	Schooner	David Rees	1880
JOHN STONARD	Schooner	James Morgan	1880
MEIRION LASS	Schooner	David Morgan	1880
ELEANOR & BETSEY	Smack	Hugh Morgan	1880
DORA ANN	Barque	John Lloyd	1881
PILGRIM	Schooner	John Davies	1882
SNOWDON	Barque	John Lewis	1882
OLIVE BRANCH	Schooner	David Jenkins	1882
ZINNIA	Barque	Evan Lewis Davies	1882
ETHEL ANN	Schooner	Abraham Davies	1883
ZIMI	Barque	David Lloyd	1886
JOHN WESLEY	Schooner	David Lewis	1886
SARAH DAVIES	Schooner	David Davies	1887
NATHANIEL	Schooner	Thomas Davies	1887
PILGRIM	Brig	Thomas Jones	1888
CATHERINE	Schooner	John Jones	1888
CATHERINE	Schooner	Richard Jones	1889
ELEANOR & JANE	Schooner	David Davies	1890
LORNE	Schooner	William Williams	1890
HOLT HILL	Barque	Richard Edwards	1891
CECIL BRINDLEY	Schooner	David Davies	1892
PLUVIER	Schooner	Thomas Davies	1892
ROSE HILL	Barque	Evan Jenkins	1893
IVANHOE	Barque	David Williams	1894

BIDSTON HILL	Barque	Evan Jenkins	1895
COROMANDEL	Barque	Lewis Williams	1895
CARADOG	Barque	Lewis Williams	1895
ANN JANE	Schooner	James Morgan	1895
ELLEN ROBERTS	Schooner	John Simon	1898
OCEAN BELLE	Snow	Richard Williams	1899

There were countless seamen other than master mariners who deserve to be remembered as they contributed significantly to Borth's rich maritime history. It seems that almost every family produced at least one master mariner, and many crew members, generation after generation. The sea also attracted newcomers to the village and their surnames suggest that the families came with the building of the railway. These include Lunt, Meddins, Bywater, George, Pierce, Brodigan and Dutton.

There follows further details of some locally owned ships commanded and often crewed by Borth men. The last entry is a vessel owned by a Liverpool shipping company which employed Borth captains at the close of the 19th century.

CHARLOTTE, 148 TONS, BRIGANTINE.

MAY 1869:

Master Richard Jones, age 28, certificate no. 32878.

The voyage was to be between Aberdyfi and Montevideo and any port on the River Plate and from there to any port in Brazil, the United States, Falkland Islands, coast of Mauritius, onto any port in the Mediterranean or continent of Europe, or any port in the Baltic and back to a final port in the U.K.

MAY 1870:

Master Richard Jones.

Voyage from Greenock to any or all West Indian islands and settlements and any port or ports of North or South America and return to U.K.

OCTOBER 1871:

Master Richard Jones.

Voyage from Greenock to any Mediterranean or Black Sea ports.

Master Richard Jones.

The voyage was to be from Glasgow to Rosario and to any port in South America, North or South Pacific, Australian colonies, India or China Sea, Mauritius, east and west coasts of Africa, West Indies, British North America, United States of America, Mediterranean Sea, Adriatic and Black Seas, until ship returns to final port of discharge on continental Europe or United Kingdom.

LORNE, 74 TONS, SCHOONER

Master John Hughes, age 40, from 1875 – 1887. He became owner in 1877.

In December 1887 John M. Hughes became master, then his father John Hughes resumed command in May 1888. Borth men were predominant amongst crew members as in one voyage in 1876:

Mate, John Jenkins, age 25
Able seaman, John Pierce age 38
Able seaman, William Jones, age 16
Able seaman, Thomas Pierce age 30

Master William Hughes in 1890 for one voyage, John Hughes once again resumed master's position until 1896. With the ownership transferred to David Davies of Aberystwyth in 1896 the Borth connection ended.

GRATITUDE, 85 TONS, SCHOONER

Master Richard Jones, age 30, was in command from September 1866 to 28th February 1867, when ship was lost on Aberdyfi bar. The ship's compliment was all from Borth, including the master Richard Jones, John James and David Davies who all survived.

FALCON, 53 TONS, SCHOONER

Master John Lewis, age 27, certificate no. 32685, was in command from 1863 to 1869. On 8th May 1868 Enoch James age 41 became owner and master until 1874. The crew was always predominantly from Borth as on one voyage in 1863 when the crew was listed as:

Master John Lewis, age 27
Mate Richard Lewis, age 25
Able seaman Thomas Lewis, age 18
Boy Evan Hughes, age 11

The Falcon traded mainly around the coast of Britain and Ireland.

CATHERINE, 16 TONS, SLOOP

This vessel was run solely by the Hughes family. It was owned by the brothers David and Hugh Hughes who took turns as skipper, and another family member Thomas Hughes crewed her. She was destroyed by fire in Porthclais Harbour in 1876, after a short working life of 12 years. A descendant of this family, John Hughes of Caenant, recalls his father being adamant that John's grandfather had purposely put a match to the sloop to gain the insurance (Hughes, pers. comm. 2003).

FRANCIS POOLE, 84 TONS, SCHOONER

Master William Lewis, age 36 was in command from 1858-1863. He unfortunately died on board the vessel in October of 1863. There was a predominance of Borth men amongst the crew, one of whom was a young David Davies born 1848, profiled in the text, who in 1866 was only an able seaman earning £2/15/- per month.

JANE OWENS, 96 TONS, SCHOONER

Master in 1863, Thomas Lewis.
Master in 1864, John Davies, aged 31, certificate no. 28838.

During this period all the crew came from Borth.

JANE SOPHIA, 78 TONS, SCHOONER

Master in 1863, John Lewis, aged 41.

Master from 1866 – 1868, James Morgan ,aged 25.

During this period the crew were predominantly from Borth.

Mate William Morgans, age 31
Able seaman Thomas Williams 21
Able seaman Richard Lewis age 19
Ships boy was Morgan Morgans age 13

From 1868 – 1870 John Lewis was master. David Davies, profiled on page 57, was on this vessel for 2 years.

MEIRION LASS, 60 TONS, SCHOONER

D.W. Morgan's father, James Morgan of Borth age 36 was master from 1877 – 1880 and his cousin David Morgan followed in 1880.

MISS EVANS, 97 TONS, SCHOONER

Master in 1863, John Rees, certificate no. 32649
Master in 1864, John Davies, certificate no. 20918
Master in 1868, Richard Davies, certificate no. 83688
Master in 1871, Thomas Davies.

This vessel was predominantly crewed by Borth men.

XANTHUS, 123 TONS, BRIGANTINE

Master from 1866 – 1868, David Jones, certificate no. 81128, with an all Borth crew
Master and owner in 1872, Hugh Morgan, certificate no. 70901, with an all Borth crew, consisting of:

Mate, John Richards.
Able Seaman, John George.
Able Seaman, John Jenkins.
Ordinary Seaman, John Edwards.

Ordinary Seaman, Thomas Davies.
Ships Boy, David Morgan.

Master in 1877, David Morgan.
Master in 1878, Evan Lewis.

SEVEN BROTHERS, 65 TONS, SCHOONER

This vessel was originally a sloop prior to it's conversion to a schooner in 1866.

Master and owner in 1870, David Morgan.
Master and owner in 1872, Thomas Morgan.
Master and owner in 1874, James Morgan.
Master and owner in 1878, David Davies, age 50, of Amity House, High Street, Borth,

CAMBRIAN, 79 TONS, SCHOONER

Master in 1873, Thomas Lewis.
Master in 1874, William Arter.
Master in 1876 ,Thomas Lewis.
Master in 1877, Thomas Lewis, with an all Borth crew consisting of:

Bosun, Arthur Lunt.
Able Seaman, John Hughes.
Ordinary Seaman, John Jones.
Ships Boy, Thomas Bywater, age 14.

By 1881 farmer Owen Owens of Dolclettwr Tre'rddol relinquished his ownership.
Master and owner in 1881, David Williams, unfortunately he died on board in 1883 and his brother Thomas took over.
Master and owner from 1884 – 1907, Thomas Williams.

SARAH AND MARY, 76 TONS, SCHOONER

Master in 1867, Richard Davies.

Master in 1868, Thomas Davies.

In 1869, 29 year old Captain John Davies of Glanwern was master and owner, he remained in this position until 1884 when there was a change of ownership. The crew on some of the voyages under Captain John Davies were, Thomas Rees, John Jones and ships boys John Thomas 15, and in 1878, George Medding also 15 years of age.

KOH-I-NOOR, 66 TONS, SCHOONER

Master in 1868, David Hughes, age 40.
Master in 1869, John Hughes, age 32.
Bosun, Thomas Hughes, age 30.
Ordinary Seaman, Thomas Richards, age 17.
Ships Boy, William Williams, age 12.

In 1870 the master John Hughes's wife died so he had to leave the ship at Bridgewater to return to Borth for the funeral, he later rejoined the ship. John Hughes remained master until 1876, and this vessel had a Borth crew continually during his time in charge.

CECIL BRINDLEY, 103 TONS, SCHOONER

This schooner was very much a Borth vessel for 40 years from 1871 – 1911.

1871 John Lewis was master, certificate no. 43226
1873 William Richards was Master, certificate no. 87303. On this voyage from Mostyn to Santander there were another three of the Richards clan aboard, John Richards, Bosun, 25 years of age, Thomas Richards O.S. 19 and Evan Richards O.S. 17.
1874 – 1877 Enoch Lewis was master, certificate no. 96262
1878 David Davies of Glanwern was master, certificate no. 25426.
The average crew totalled six and were primarily Borth men, and on one memorable voyage to the Baltic under Captain Davies, the whole of the ship's compliment were of the Davies clan:

Master, David Davies, age 40.
Mate, John Davies.
Able Seaman, David Davies, age 26.
Ordinary Seaman, James Davies, age 19.
Ships Boy, Richard Davies, age 14.

Truly a ship's compliment made up of Teulu Sion Dafydd!

From 1885 Captain David Davies of Glanwern and John Frances were joint owners. In 1890 John Frances relinquished his share and Captain Davies continued until he ceased ownership of the *Cecil Brindley* in 1911 which ended this vessel's 40 year old link with Borth. From that time she was under Irish ownership and was finally abandoned at Dublin in 1923

DRUSUS, 374 TONS, BARQUE

Built in Sunderland in September 1857, with an eliptical stern and male figurehead.

Transferred from Newcastle on 26th March 1879.

Registered in Aberystwyth on 27th March 1879, official number: 20253.

Master/Owner David Rees, Gloucester House, Borth. Master mariners certificate no. 11460.

In February 1880 the tonnage was changed to 398 tons.

In August 1881 David Rees died and ownership was transferred to his widow Elizabeth Rees, Gloucester House, Borth. Mrs Rees mortgaged the ship for £280.

The joint mortgagees were:
Margaret Thomas, wife of John Thomas, a farmer at Tanyrallt, and Ann Davies, wife of Hugh Davies of Talybont.

The vessel was sold at Rosario by order of the Federal Judge to satisfy claims of the creditors in August 1883, as per letter from the Vice Consul. Register closed and certificate of registry cancelled on 8th November 1883.

HOLT HILL, 2,268 TONS, BARQUE

This vessel; built in Glasgow in 1890 by Russel and Co, was a 282 foot long four masted sailing barque. The owners were the, Sailing Ship "Holt Hill" Company Ltd. of 58 South John Street, Liverpool.
Master from 1890-92: Richard Edwards, born 1851, of Glanwern, Borth.

Master from 1893-96; Evan Jenkins, born 1859, of Borth. Captain Jenkins also commanded the *Rose Hill* from 1889-92, and the *Bidston Hill* in 1898.

57. Nerissa, Schooner, Captain David Jenkins

58. Charlotte, Brigantine, Captain Richard Jones

59. Catherine, Schooner, Captain John Richards

60. Dovey Belle, Schooner, Captain John James

61. Jane Jones, Schooner, Captain John Jones

62. Island Maid, Brigantine, William Jones

63. Lorne, Schooner, Captain John Hughes

64. Caradog, Barque, Captain Lewis Williams

65. Catherine Morgan, Schooner, Captain John Jones

66. The wreck of the Sloop John and Mary

SU MMARY

It is remarkable that so small a collection of dwellings straggling from the southern high ground and along the stone strand, that was Borth, should have existed centuries ago and been mentioned in 1373. It is probably even older than that date but its beginnings are lost in myth and legend eluding those who attempt to determine exactly when it began. It was not until the beginning of the 19th century that there was some definite record of what constituted Borth. Then, it consisted of the 2 farms; Brynowen and Pengoitan, 2 houses, 2 boat houses and around 80 cottages.

Census data indicates that the economy of the village increasingly improved during the 19th century. This is reflected in the growing numbers of trade and business people, alongside a decrease in paupers from the 14 listed in 1841 to none in 1871. The advent of postal services by 1851 meant new job opportunities. There were to be more varied occupations such as hoteliers, platelayers, cooks and grooms, after the arrival of the railway in 1864. Even so, seafaring was still the main form of employment. It has been estimated that during the last two centuries over one thousand men from Borth became seafarers.

When the days of sail and local export had declined, Borth mariners had to seek work elsewhere. Liverpool, Middlesborough, Manchester, Cardiff, Swansea and Barry became the main ports of employment. This situation meant that inevitably some would move to live permanently at these locations. Borth's dependence on the sea to provide a livelihood was by the early 20th century being supplemented by the holiday industry. After World War II, the shipping industry of Britain went into sharp decline, and in the last 50 years has decreased to a present that sees few Borth people in maritime employment. Thus, Borth's existence has until the middle of the 20th century been irrevocably linked to seafaring; since then it has been involved with the tourist industry. The latter, however, has not provided the levels of employment that the former did, nor has it provided many opportunities for local investment.

Dr. Reginald Davies has compiled a Welsh Mariners' Index that mainly lists officers and includes; 2nd Mates, 1st Mates, Ships Engineers and Captains covering the period 1845-1945. Currently there are in excess of 20,000 individuals mentioned. From this formidable research one can appreciate Ceredigion's contribution to the maritime history of Wales by perusing the following figures. Added to the information from Dr. R. Davies' data are a further 52 Borth captains from my own researches.

New Quay - 661, Cardigan - 539, Aberystwyth - 434, Aberaeron - 373, Borth - 301, Aberporth - 156, Llangrannog - 118, Aberarth - 58, Llanon - 22, Llanrhystud - 13.

Historian Lewis Lloyd's remarks about Borth being the lifeblood of Aberdyfi are born out, as the figures for that port are only 93. What emerges from this is that Borth, a village without a harbour, made an outstanding contribution to the maritime history of Wales in relation to its size and… certainly compared with that of any other village in Ceredigion.

This work is a tribute to all those from Borth who made their living on, or from the sea. They deserve to be remembered not only by their descendants worldwide, but also by those who are now living in Borth. Today's residents have inherited an amazing legacy, which I hope they appreciate.

BIBLIOGRAPHY

Anonymous, *Llanfihangel Geneu'r Glyn, Parochial Records*, Vol.1, p.91, 12 August 1728, manuscripts, National Library of Wales, Aberystwyth

Bannerman, Nigel, 'Fish Trap Types', *Maritime Wales*, no.21, 2000

Baring-Gould, S. & Fisher, J. *The Lives of the British Saints*, London, 1908

Beadnell, Dr. Herbert, *An Extraordinary Guide to the City of Borth*, Stretton Press, Church Stretton Salop, 1920

Breverton, T.D. *The Book of Welsh Saints*, Glyndwr Publishing, Bro Morgannwg, 2000

Bromwich, Rachel, *Dafydd ap Gwilym*, Gomer Press, Wales, 1993

Buckland, Frank & Walpole, Spencer, *Report on the Seafisheries of England and Wales*, 1878/9 Parliamentary Papers, vol. XV11, Manuscript, National Library of Wales, Aberystwyth

Campbell-Jones, Susan, Shipbuilding at New Quay Cardiganshire 1779-1878, *Ceredigion*, vol 7, 1975

Colyer, R.J. 'The Enclosure and Drainage of Cors Fochno (Borth bog) 1813-1847', *Journal of the Ceredigion Antiquarian Society*, vol. viii, 1976-79

Conran, T, Welsh Verse, W. B. C. Books, Bridgend, 1999

Costigan, N.G. et al. *Cyfres Beirdd y Tywysogion*, Cyfrol v1, Gwasg Prifysgol Cymru, Caerdydd, 1995

Davies, John, *A History of Wales*, Penguin Books, London, 1993

Davies, John, Susan and Aveianah 'Recollections of a Master Mariner From Borth, Cardiganshire', *Dyfed Family History Society, V (1)*, National Library of Wales, Aberystwyth, 1994

Davies, J.L. & Kirby, D.P. (eds), *Cardiganshire County History*, vol.1, University Press of Wales, 1994

Davies, R.R., *The Age of Conquest, Wales* 1063-1415, Oxford University Press, 1987

Davies, Stanley, 'Cardiganshire Salt Smugglers', *Archaeologia Cambrensis 91*, National Library of Wales, Aberystwyth, 1936

Davies, Walter, *General View of Agriculture and Domestic Economy of North Wales*, Richard Phillips, London, 1810

Davies, Walter, *General View of Agriculture and Domestic Economy of South Wales*, vol.2, Macmillan, Covent Garden, 1815

Enoch, Randall Evans, *Llanfihangel Genau'r Glyn*, Cambrian Printers, Aberystwyth, 2002

Gascoine, C.P., *The Story of the Cambrian*, Woodall, Minshall and Thomas, Wrexham, 1922

Gater, Dilys, *The Battles of Wales*, Gwasg Carreg Gwalch, Llanrwst 1991

Gater, Dilys, *Historic Wrecks of Wales*, Gwasg Carreg Gwalch, Llanrwst 1992

Graves, Robert, *The White Goddess*, Faber and Faber Ltd, London, 1971

Grimble, A.D., *The Salmon Rivers of England and Wales*, K.P. Trench, Trubner and co. London, 1913

Guest, Lady Charlotte, *The Mabinogion*, Dover Publications Inc. New York, 1997

Hughes, D.T. (Rev). 'Looking Back', *Cambrian News*, April-Dec.1947

Holland, D, *Bygones*, Gwasg Carreg Gwalch, Wales, 1992

Jenkins, David, 'A Borth Shipwreck', *Journal of the Cardiganshire Anitquarian Society*, vol.1, Gowerian Press, 1950-51

Jenkins, Geraint, H. & Jones Ieuan Gwynedd, (eds). *Cardiganshire County History*, vol.3, University Press of Wales, Cardiff, 1998

Jenkins, Geraint, H. Lewis Morris, 'The Fat Man of Cardiganshire', *Ceredigion*, vol.X1V, no.2, 2002

Jenkins, J.Geraint, 'Herring Fishing in Wales', *Maritime Wales*, no.4, 1979

Jenkins, J.G. *The Inshore Fishermen of Wales*, University of Wales Press, Cardiff, 1991

Jenkins, J.G. *Maritime Heritage*, Gomer Press, Dyfed, 1982

Jenkins, J.T., *The Herring and the Herring Fisheries*, P.S. King and Son, London, 1927

Jones, G. & Jones, T. *The Mabinogion*, J.M. Dent& Sons Ltd. London, 1976

Jones, Thomas, *Brut y Tywysogion*, Red Book of Hergest version, 1955

Kirby, D.P., 'The Place of Ceredigion in the Early History of Wales circa 400-1170', *Journal of the Cardiganshire Antiquarian Society*, vol.1, no.2, 1970

Kurlansky, Mark, *Cod*, Vintage Books, Griffin Press, Australia, 1999

Lewis, W.J., 'The Cwmsymlog Lead Mine', *Ceredigion*, Vol.2, 1952-55

Lloyd, Lewis, *A Real Little Seaport, The Port of Aberdyfi and Its People*. 1565-1920, vol.1, Gwasg Pantycelyn, Gwynedd, 1996

Lloyd, Lewis, *A Real Little Seaport, The Port of Aberdyfi and its People*. 1565-1920, vol. 2, Gwasg Pantycelyn, Gwynedd, 1996

Lloyd, R.J.H., 'Aberystwyth Fishing Boats', *Mariner's Mirror*, vol.41, no.2, 1955

Lord, Peter, *The Visual Culture of Wales; Imaging the Nation*, University of Wales Press, Cardiff, 2000

Macdonald, T., *The White Lanes of Summer*, Macmillan, London, 1975

Morgan, Gerald, *North Cardiganshire Shipbuilding 1700-1800,* University College of Wales, Aberystwyth, 1992

Morgan, D.W., *Brief Glory,* The Brython Press, Liverpool, 1948

Morgan, D.W., 'Taliesin and the Borth Weir', *Borth Review 2,* 1950

North, F.J., *Sunken Cities,* University of Wales Press, Cardiff, 1957

Owens, B.G., 'Gwir Iforiaid Castell Gwallter', *Ceredigion vol.111* pp. 24-29, 1956-59

Parry, Thomas, (ed), *The Oxford Book of Welsh Verse,* Clarendon Press, Oxford, 1995

Penrice & Margam Estate Papers, *A List of Seafaring Men Boatmen and Bargemen From the County of Cardigan,* taken the 18th day of May 1678, Manuscript no. 3277, National Library of Wales, Aberystwyth

Raw-Rees, D., *Borth and Ynyslas Golf Club,* The Cambrian News Ltd. 1986

Rees, D.M. *Historical Industrial Scenes: Wales,* Moorland Publishing, London, 1980

Richards, A.E. *Home For Good,* Short Story, unpublished, author's collection, 1946

Richards, A.E. *Who'll Buy My Fresh Herrings,* author's collection, 1948, play for voices performed 27/12/1957

Richards, A.E., *Harvesting Herring,* short story, unpublished, author's collection, 1947

Richards, A.E., *Master Mariner,* play for voices, author's collection, 1953

Samuel, D., 'Cwm Cynfelin and Llangorwen Church', *Cardiganshire Antiquarian Society, Transactions and Archaelogical Record,* vol 1, no.4, Bridge Press, Lampeter, 1914

Smylie, Mike, *The Herring Fisheries of Wales,* Gwasg Carreg Gwalch, 1998

Stammers, M.K., 'The Welsh Sloop', *Maritime Wales,* no.21, 2000

Stephens, T., 'The Poems of Taliesin', *Archaeologia Cambrensis,* vol.2, National Library of Wales, 1851

Stephens, T., 'The Poems of Taliesin', no. V11, *Archaelogia Cambrensis,* vol 6, 1853

Thomas, Dylan Marlais, *The Collected Poems of Dylan Thomas 1934-1952,* New Directions Publishing Corporation, New York, 1957

Thomas, Gwyn, *Dafydd ap Gwilym his poems,* University of Wales Press, Cardiff, 2001

Thomas, T. Wynne, *Dovey Ferry, Its History and Associations,* Reprinted from the Cambrian News, 23/8/1929 and Aberdovey Guide 1864

Thomas, T. Wynne, *History & Survey of the Trinity Port of Aberdovey,* The Cambrian News Ltd. Aberystwyth, 1947

Thorpe, Lewis, *Gerald of Wales The Journey Through Wales/The Description Of Wales,* Penguin Classics, London, 1978

Troughton William, *Aberystwyth Harbour, An Illustrated History,* National Library of Wales, Aberystwyth, 1997

Vaughan, A.C., 'Correspondence to Glyn Davies, Sept 19th 1913', *Manuscript 644,* National Library of Wales, Aberystwyth

Williams, Richard, *Limekilns and Limeburning,* Shire Publications, Haverfordwest, 1989

ILLUSTRATIONS

36. Anonymous, *Jac "Shami" Davies Mackerel Fishing off Carreg Felin*, circa 1912, private collection
37. Anonymous, *Jack "Shami" Davies the Younger in dragnetting Clothes, with Bass,* circa 1950, private collection
38. *The Barred Haven,* Topographical Prints of Cardiganshire, National Library of Wales
39. Anonymous, *Borth Dragnetters,* photograph, circa 1930, private collection
40. Welsh Primitive watercolour, *Rocks at Aberystwyth,* circa 1850
41. Anonymous, *Tom Hughes and his Mother Outside Castle Stores,* circa 1910, private collection
42. Anonymous, *Mr Jenkins of Pengoitan with young Ted Richards at Twll Ladi Wen,* circa 1911
43. Anonymous, *Will Sion Dafydd,* 1840
44. Anonymous, *David Davies Balmoral House, With Handcraft for Fish,* photograph, circa 1935, private collection
45. Anonymous, *Jac Richards with Lobster,* circa 1978, private collection
46. Anonymous, *Captain David Davies in his Old Age Repairing Boat,* circa 1915
47. Captain David Jenkins, *Seaman's Delight,* 1907
48. Anonymous, *Captain William Richards and his Wife Anne With Their Four Children,* circa 1890, private collection. Back left to right: David Edward, Peggy, John Thomas and Elizabeth
49. Anonymous, *Borth Captains,* circa 1890
50. Anonymous, *Borth Captains,* circa 1890, with the names of their ships. Back row left to right: H. Hughes *The Dart,* J. Evans *Savatele,* W. Jones *Picton,* R. Jones *Charlotte,* J. Hughes *Lorne,* David Rees *Sabrina,* John Francis *Eleanor Francis.* Front row: D. Hughes *Friendship,* John Hughes *Jane Martha,* John Edwards *Reform,* T. Davies *Venus,* William Jones *Panthea* and John Richards *Catherine*
51. Anonymous, *Borth Captains and Lady,* circa 1890. Back row: Fourth from left, Captain David Davies
52. Anonymous, *Borth Captains,* circa 1910. Front row seated: Captain Jones Maesarfor, and far right Captain William Richards Maelgwyn
53. Anonymous, *Native Captains, Borth,* circa 1900. Front row left to right: Thomas Davies, James Davies, John Rees, Tom Rees, Captain Davies (Glenrosa House) and Captain William Williams. Back row: Captain David Jones (No.3 Saint Albans) and Captain Lewis (Cambrian Villa)
54. Anonymous, *Captains Thomas Davies and John Jones*
55. Anonymous, *Crew of the Eira,* 1888
56. Anonymous, *Crew of the Glanhafren,* 1894 (NLW photo album 2145199600085)
57. Anonymous, *Nerissa,* circa 1880
58. Anonymous, *Charlotte,* circa 1880
59. Anonymous, *Catherine,* circa 1878
60. Anonymous, *Dovey Belle,* circa 1880
61. Anonymous, *Jane Jones,* circa 1858
62. Anonymous, *Island Maid,* circa 1853
63. Anonymous, *Lorne,* circa 1880
64. Anonymous, *Caradog,* circa 1900, (NLW photo album 1392, PZ 5926/75)
65. Anonymous, *Catherine Morgan,* circa 1860
66. Welsh Primitive, *John and Mary,* circa 1848